iGO

INTERNATIONAL ASSOCIATION OF GOVERNMENT OFFICIALS

Representing the finest clerks, recorders, election officials & treasurers.

"Rarely does your instinct tell you to do the wrong thing first."

...Pamela

This book is for you.

Rave reviews . . . .

“I read your book over the weekend. It’s a well written piece of work, a story worthy of being rolled into a John Grisham novel or a Leonardo DiCaprio movie.” **Mark Kolman, Audit Manager and Member of IIA**

“I read the first 130 pages of your book before I went to bed. After an hour of unsuccessfully trying to sleep, I got up and finished the book. It reminded me a bit of the Grisham book, The King of Torts. I could certainly see incorporating your book into the classroom in future semesters.”
Warren Bostrom, Assistant Professor, College of St. Benedict / St. John's University

"I just finished reading your book and wanted to thank you for taking the time to put your intimate experiences on paper. That, in itself takes courage and I highly commend you for that. I am recommending all of my loan officers, processors and entire staff to read it and be mindful of the consequences of fraud and how easy it is to participate in it."
Mark Duplantis, LA Divisional Manager, Charter Funding

"Just a few moments ago I finished reading the last page of your book and I have to tell you, it's amazing. I just wanted to say thank you for being that "willing person" who has been down a road that none of us want to go down."
Belinda Evans, Flag Bank

Diary of a White Collar Criminal

Jerome Mayne

Table of Contents

Prologue

Just this morning, all across America, hundreds of professionals woke up, ate breakfast and got ready for work. But they're not at the office right now. In fact, no one has expected them at the office in years. Because, at exactly 8:00 a.m. they reported to the maintenance shed for grounds-keeping duty, or to the utility closet and got a mop and a bucket – today they get to clean stairway number 4. The luckier ones will report to the education department where they'll get to use a tiny portion of their brains teaching drug dealers how to read.

Tonight, they'll go to bed on a thin plastic mattress and lie awake for hours counting the years, months, weeks, days, hours – I remember counting the minutes until I was released from federal prison.

In 1989 I graduated from the paralegal program at UCLA and worked in business litigation for three years. A couple of years later I switched careers and took up employment as a mortgage loan officer. My first job in the world of finance was at Countrywide Funding in Pasadena, California.

In 1993 I relocated with my wife and newborn son to my home state of Minnesota and took a job as a loan officer at Norwest Mortgage. In 1996 I started my own mortgage company, Mayne Mortgage Corp. By mid-year 1998 I had 10 employees; my company was growing.

I was the self-proclaimed "Entrepreneur of the '90s".

In December 1998 I was indicted by federal prosecutors and charged with conspiracy to commit mail fraud, wire fraud and money laundering — a crime that took place four years earlier, in 1994, while I was at Norwest.

In September 1999 I received a 21-month prison sentence for these crimes.

On November 4, 1999, I reported to the federal prison in Yankton, South Dakota.

For the next two years I was federal inmate number 08657-041. To most of my business partners and employees, I became the guy they couldn't be associated with anymore – guilt by association is very real. To my family and friends, I became the son, brother or friend they *thought* they knew. To any potential employer, I was a felon - an ex-convict. To my kids, I've always been Dad. Thank God, youth and innocence never judge.

I have never been an award winning business man, nor do I have any scholarly credentials to put after my name. I didn't complete college. My achievements in the business world are quite trivial, compared to the men and women I now meet speaking at conferences and conventions.

Apparently, I'm not even a good criminal. I am definitely not a hero.

So, why read what I have to say?

Because once, I was you.

Chapter 1

Evolution of a Felon

February 1, 1993

Karen and I are moving back to Minnesota. I have a lead on a loan officer job at Norwest Mortgage right there in St. Paul. I'm a little nervous about being on full commission since the past two years I received a salary at my loan officer job at Countrywide in Pasadena, California. We also have a lead on a town home in Woodbury. The rent isn't too bad. It'll be perfect for our little family. I'm flying back there this week to secure the job and the town home.

March 16, 1993

I am truly a salesman now. Or at least I'm going to have to be. I already know all about mortgages and guidelines, so I really don't need training on that. It's all about sales! My boss is training a couple of us new guys on sales techniques. At Countrywide all my business was handed to me. Here, I have to go out and find it. I eat what I kill. It's all about getting people to refer business to me. Real estate agents, financial planners, attorneys (I know a few of them) and accountants. I also have to tap my "sphere of influence;" meaning, my family and friends. It'll be a challenge, that's for sure. I really like my boss. In a way, he feels like a father figure. Stern yet calm. He's willing to take us new guys under his wing and show us how to get business, instead of just telling us to go out there and sell, sell, sell!

Karen and I are set to get married this fall. Our families are happy, especially her dad.

June 23, 1993

I've been getting quite a few loans in the door. They're refinance loans instead of loans to purchase a home. They're mostly coming from people I know. I've also met a couple real estate agents who have given me a couple deals. I haven't done many purchase transactions, so I don't feel like I know what I'm doing there. It's still all about sales and building relationships. It's hard to put extra time into this job when I have a family, but I'm going to have to figure something out. We can't survive on

Karen's pay from her administrative assistant position. I can't sit around for one minute because I know that sales activity equals sales results. That's what my boss says.

People are cool here at work and I get along with them very well. I thought that I'd be hanging out with my old buddies when we moved back here to Minnesota. I do, but I spend much more time with the people I work with. We go to happy hours and Twins games and stuff like that.

July 7, 1993

We found a house! It's less than a block from the office. I think we'll qualify for a loan, but since I just started on this commission income, and the guidelines say that a borrower earning commission income has to have a two year history of it, I won't be able to help get us qualified. Karen's income should be fine. She should be able to qualify for an FHA loan. I can't be the loan officer on it. For one thing, I don't know anything about FHA loans. I need to find out for sure, but not on this one. Secondly, my boss said that I shouldn't be the loan officer on transactions where I have an interest. I guess it has something to do with me possibly having the temptation to cut corners in the approval process. They're his rules so I guess I'll follow them.

Speaking of rules, there's a guy here at work who is working on a loan, and he himself signed a verification of employment form for his customer. It was sent out to the employer of this borrower and it came back all filled out, but the employer forgot to sign it.

I know it's wrong to sign someone else's name on a legal document. I know it is. Maybe it's just different around here. I'm not going to say anything. I'm the new guy and I'm still learning how things work. After all, *I'm* not the one breaking the rules.

August 5, 1993

I've been getting referrals from a lot of agents. I'm still doing a lot of refinance business and I'm glad since they're so much easier. My boss says we'll need to focus on purchase business because when rates go up, the refinance loan business will go away. I understand. But I'm finally making real money! I got a commission check for over eight grand! This will come in handy for the October wedding. Boy, that's coming up fast.

Timmy is showing signs of walking and he's not even one year old! Oh, and I'm starting to like the movie *Aladdin*! Gonna get me one of them lamps.

September 19, 1993

It's great to be a homeowner, but yard work isn't as much fun as I thought it would be. Furnishing a home isn't cheap either. There are a lot of expenses involved in getting married and the wedding is coming up in about two weeks. Oh, my God. I'm getting married!

I started working with a great new loan program they have here. It's offered through Norwest Bank and it's called the Community Home Ownership Program. They call it CHOP for short. It's for low-income/first-time homebuyers. It's a little harder to put together than an FHA loan because it has such quirky guidelines. I'm going to make myself an expert on it because no other loan officers like to do CHOP loans. I came up with a flyer for it. The catch line reads, "Having trouble with tough loans? Let me take a crack at it with my CHOP loan."

October 10, 1993

The wedding went fine. How could it have gone wrong with all the planning that went into it? It's a relief now that the pressure from Karen's father is gone. He's happy that we're married and that I have a job where I make a lot of money to take care of his little girl. The road ahead looks good.

A few weeks ago I decided to make my own music CD. I think I picked the right musicians to play and produce it. The studio time will only cost $2,000 to record ten songs. That's an awesome deal for me! It'll be great finally having my own CD. I'm not really sure what I'll do with it when I'm done. It's not like I have a band and can tour. I can't take time away from work. At least I'll have a recording of ten of the best songs I've written over the past 11 years.

January 12, 1994

November and December were hard for business. People just don't want to apply for loans when the holidays are approaching. Sure, there was a business slowdown during the holidays when I worked at Countrywide, but not quite like this one, and I also had a salary in addition to my commission.

Karen and I spent too much money over the holidays. My boss acknowledges that there is a business slowdown, but he doesn't let us use that as an excuse. He says that when business slows down, it just means you need to work that much harder. I understand, but I just wasn't ready. It's my fault that I didn't just buck up. Well, it's a new year. It's time to kick some butt!

Chapter 2

Two Miltons

March 21, 1994

I'm beginning to regret becoming an expert on the community outreach/low income loans. "Hi, my niche is working with low-income/first-time homebuyers where the loan amounts are lower and the commissions are less." Whatever!!!! I have to admit that even though the commissions are lower, I do like the challenge of these complicated loans. I have accepted the fact that the customers of low-income loans usually have pretty tough credit. I usually have to dig up monthly payment histories for stuff like pagers or rented furniture through Rent-a-Center. Those are still monthly payments, but trying to convince the underwriters of that is quite a different thing. I think I have a good system. I know the underwriters, and they know they can expect a fight from me on behalf of my borrowers.

I have six primary real estate agents who refer business to me and four or five new agents who say they'll give me a few buyers to see how I do. Not bad after just one year as a fully commissioned loan officer.

Tonight was a good family night. We ate pizza. Timmy doesn't know it yet, but this will probably be his favorite food someday. Like, maybe when he's two?

March 22, 1994

Today, I got a call from Mike. He rocks. Right now, he's my best referring real estate agent. He gave me two people to pre-qualify. He also gave my name to a real estate investor who actually called me. His name is Milt May and he said that he buys and sells a lot of houses in the low-income areas; my niche!

He's awesome. He also said he needs a good loan officer to send his buyers to. Ahh that would be me! He says that, at first, there will be a lot of people to pre-qualify. Who cares if they're pre-quals? I'm sure they'll turn into real deals eventually.

Married life is going well. Not one fight yet. Everything is still going great with the new house. The location has turned out to be amazing, just a block away from the office. The only problem is that I find myself running home all the time to see Timmy. How am I supposed to stay away from my baby boy?

April 2, 1994

God, I felt like a wizard today. I'm one of the only guys in the office who has a laptop. I designed a spreadsheet that calculates loan payments and closing costs. It even has the Norwest logo. It's perfect for open houses. I sold a copy of this spreadsheet program to Clinton for thirty bucks. Now I'm a software developer! I wonder if I have to claim that on my taxes.

I've been playing piano a lot more lately. Not really writing anything new. I'm mostly just playing and practicing my old songs. Any time I play Elton John songs, I just think of Jeff. The recording of my CD is going very slow. It's hard to find the time to get down there. Then when I do find the time, Derrick and Mave have someone else in their studio. I think I might buy a drum set.

April 21, 1994

My new awesome referral source Milt, has been sending me a ton of borrowers. They're all prequals, but what the hell, they'll turn eventually. He told me yesterday that he thinks I'll be the best loan officer he's ever worked with. Oh, yeah! Of course I am!

I gave Milt the list of what the borrowers need to bring to the loan application appointments, but these people bring practically nothing. One thing Milt made very clear, since the people he is sending me are his customers, he wants me to call him right away if I need any additional information. Not too out of the ordinary, some of the real estate agents I work with have the same rules.

I wonder if I'm ever going to meet Milt in person? He says he lives in Atlanta, but purchases a lot of properties here in the Twin Cities. He told me I should come down there sometime. He sure calls me a lot.

May 5, 1994

Karen and I had dinner tonight at Dixie's on Grand Avenue in St. Paul. The restaurant was recommended by Milty. Is he the man or what?

Anyhow, sometimes I feel like Karen and I are just roommates who share a child. It works out great. I suppose I'm in love. I mean, I'd know if I didn't love her wouldn't I? I'm not sure if she loves me. We both love Timmy.

May 23, 1994

Met with Josh today; one of the first real borrowers from Milt. This kid said that he didn't know where he works! He said that he wasn't even sure what his hourly wage was. Where does Milt find these people? I called Milt after the guy left, just like I'm supposed to do, and asked why this guy wouldn't know where he works or know his own hourly wage.

Of course Milt had an explanation. He said that Josh has been working for his uncle for the past 3 years and that his uncle just incorporated his company recently. Hence, Josh's confusion. Yeah, right. He also said that sometimes his buyers are a little sensitive about their financial information and said he'll get the info for me. That's fine; this way I don't have to go and chase it down.

Anyhow, I told Milt that Josh thought he made about $8 - $9 an hour. So he said that I might have confused Josh when I asked if it was gross or net pay. Even though I don't believe anyone is so stupid that they don't know where they work or how much they make an hour, I told Milt that this hourly wage would still not be enough to qualify him for the loan. Milt seemed surprised and then asked me how much someone would need to make per hour in order to qualify for a $76,500 loan. What a stupid question. I told him it would have to be at least $13.75 an hour. If Milt's going to be in this business, he should learn how to run a financial calculator.

May 25, 1994

One of Milt's associates dropped off Josh's W2's and pay stubs today and what do you know—he makes $13.75 an hour. What am I supposed to do now? It's awfully fishy, but I can't accuse Milt of cooking up fake documents. I could probably get sued or something for accusing someone of this kind of thing. Not only that, but he'd probably never use me again as a loan officer. I mean, they look real. Could Milt have actually made these? He doesn't seem that sophisticated, but I suppose he could have. He must have. I mean, it's not my job to run around and verify the authenticity of every document I get, is it?

Nonetheless, I haven't done anything wrong – I didn't cook up any documents. And it's not like he winked at me and said, "Hey Jerome, here are the fake ones. Go forth young man and commit that fraud." Maybe the underwriter will catch it and decline the loan. I must admit, this situation has become pretty weird.

May 30, 1994

Josh's loan should be closing at the end of this week. But I doubt it will now because he doesn't have traditional credit. I can't believe how much extra work there is with Milt's borrowers.

It wouldn't be so complicated if they had debts that show up on their credit report—like credit cards. But because they don't have traditional credit, I have to track down places where they've made regular monthly payments. Then I have to verify the payments. Then I have to write a letter of explanation to the underwriter as to why they don't have traditional credit. Josh is supposed to write the letter, but it's easier to do it myself because Josh will never understand what the underwriter wants to see in this letter of explanation. Then, after all that,

I'll still have to fight with the underwriter for one reason or another because inevitably there will be some quirky thing wrong with the loan. Milt has no idea how hard I work.

As if things weren't bad enough, Milt doesn't even do the things he's supposed to do as a seller. For instance, the appraiser called for a closet to be installed so he can legally appraise the property as a three-bedroom house. Is Milt going to do it? Of course not! A licensed contractor needs do it, and his handyman Jim, is not licensed. I have a sneaky suspicion of what Milt is going to do. He's going to doctor up an invoice on some letterhead for handyman Jim. I hope he, at least, puts a logo on the letterhead.

June 13, 1994

Business is good, but I'm having a hard time keeping up with my other referral sources. I find that I'm ignoring the other loans in my pipeline because Milt sends me so many damn pre-quals.

I'm also getting to meet a lot more of Milt's associates. It's hard to keep everybody straight. There's Milt May and his best friend, Milton Marlin – the guy who dropped of Josh's pay stubs. Then there's Milton Marlin's brother Rod Marlin and his girlfriend – I can never remember her name. Then Milt has another brother and sister or something.

They all call me about twenty times a day on my pager, cell phone, work phone, and even my home phone. I never should have given them my home number. Milt calls the house and talks to Karen for five or ten minutes before he talks to me. I mean he's a super-nice guy and everything, but geez.

The receptionist at the office says Milt is rude when he calls. That makes no sense to me. He calls a lot, but he's always pretty cool with me. Anyway, I think he's a good guy and everything, but please, leave me alone and let me do my job. And talk about loans from hell; I do more work on each of his loans than I usually do on ten loans. Milt is like a high-maintenance real estate agent and he's not even licensed.

Milt says he makes a lot of money buying houses low and selling high. Maybe I should be doing that? Anyway, thank God I've got some non-Milt gravy loans in the pipeline. I can't ignore those. Milt says that Milton is going to meet me downtown tomorrow after the closing to have cocktails with me and my pals, before we go to the Twins game. Whatever.

June 14, 1994

I went to the Josh closing today. I have never seen anything like it in my entire loan officer career. It was absolute chaos. First of all, Josh didn't bring the gift funds, cash to close, he was told to bring. Somehow the homeowner's insurance binder got lost or was never obtained. Milt assured me yesterday that he would take care of getting all the required items. So I had to do a lot of scrambling to make everything work. But these were not the most remarkable events of the closing.

I was in the room when they closed the loan for my borrower Josh. Of course Norwest wired the loan money Josh was borrowing to the title company. The title company cut a check to the seller, Tamika (not Milt). She is another one of Milt's associates. The check was for somewhere around $76,000, roughly the selling price of the home. This was all fine; that was normal. But after Josh's loan closed, the closer asked me if I was going to sit in on the other closing. I had no idea what she was talking about. I figured, what the hell!

What I sat in on was a closing on the same property, only this transaction was with a seller named Gillmore Prattington. He was this old guy. Nice as hell. Anyhow, he was selling this same house to Tamika (now a buyer) for $34,500. This was a cash transaction. Tamika wasn't getting a loan to buy the house from Gillmore, she had to come up with the $34,500 in cash. But since the title company just cut a check to Tamika for about $76,000 in the other room, all she had to do was sign that check back over to the title company, and they issued a check to Gillmore for roughly $33,000 (the sale price of the home minus closing costs and earnest money). Then the title company gave Tamika a check for the difference. I sat around after everyone left so I could talk to my closer. She explained what just happened.

Basically, Gillmore, the original owner, and original seller of the property sold his house to Tamika for $34,500. Then she sold it to Josh for $76,000. Tamika got a check for $42,000, which was the difference between what she bought it for and what she sold it for. The only weird part was – this happened in reverse order.

My closer told me that as long as both transactions take place on the same day it all balances out. Even though Tamika technically sold her interest in the property to Josh before she actually had it, at the end of the day, all purchase and sale transactions were complete.

The transactions are not "time stamped" so as long as everything is cool by the end of the day, it's fine. She said that she did not prefer to close loans this way, but it was not illegal. She assured me that she would never let anyone (Tamika, Josh or Gillmore) walk out of that closing before all the checks were cut and more importantly, not before all the paperwork was signed.

I have to admit, I am very intrigued.

On the way home I called Milt and told him that I just figured out his brilliant technique, but something still concerned me. I didn't understand how Tamika could sell a house to someone before she had actually taken possession. He said it's a legal loophole that not many people know about. Apparently, once you have an agreement with a property owner to purchase his property (the purchase agreement), you then have certain rights. One of them is the right to sell your interest in the property. The original seller cannot sell it to someone else because he is legally bound to sell it to you for the price on the purchase agreement. There are other rights you don't have until after the closing, such as entering the home and stuff like that. But Milt puts that as an addendum to the purchase agreement so he can show the house to *his* potential buyers before he closes. How cool!

June 15, 1994

Okay now this was weird. I was downtown at the Loon tonight having cocktails with my buddies before we went to the Twins game and Milt's associate, Milton stopped in. Just before he left, he slid $100 to the middle of the table and said "You did a good job on Josh's loan." for doing such a good job on Josh's loan. Then he got up and left. Why the hell did he have to go and do that! Technically, it's probably not right. I mean, I know I'm not supposed to accept money from clients, but he's not technically a client. And what's the difference between him giving me $100 and him picking up $100 bar tab for me and my friends? It's not like it's illegal. Is it? What was I supposed to do – chase him down and give him back his money?

There is one curiosity that I can finally put to rest. When I first started working with them, I thought it was possible that Milt and Milton were the same person. But now I know they're different. While I was having cocktails with Milton, Milt called. I guess Milton is getting married. Since Milt is his best friend, he'll probably be in the wedding or at least at the wedding. Maybe I'll see the two Miltons at the wedding – if I'm invited.

July 8, 1994

Nicole, another one of Milt's customers I've been working with, has become a nightmare. She called me today to give me her new work number. Nice move genius. I told her right up front she's not supposed to change jobs during the loan approval process; certainly not three days before the closing!

Milt freaked out when I called and told him that we have to postpone the closing until we verify her new employment. I mean, he went ballistic!

Apparently he doesn't understand basic underwriting guidelines. When a borrower changes jobs during the approval process, their new job has to be verified because it's possible that they got fired and took a job that pays less or that the new job isn't as likely to continue as the job that *was* verified. He thinks that we shouldn't have to verify her new job because she was a nurse at her old job and she's still a nurse now, at her new job. Yeah, that's great you think that, Milt. He said that a nurse is a nurse is a nurse—they all make about the same amount of money.

Yeah, I know and I think the underwriter would be okay with it too but it still has to be verified. He said that it's no big deal because the loan is already approved and they'll never know that she has a new job. *They'll never know?* I told him that *I* know she has a new job, so therefore it has to be verified. Then he asked me whose side I was on.

I had to pull my car over when he said that because I realize now that the lines have become blurry. I politely reminded him that I worked for the bank, and have responsibilities. He mentioned that there was a great deal of borrower referrals that some other loan officer would love to have. This was obviously a threat. Now what am I supposed to do?

I am truly convinced that the borrower is a nurse at her new job and besides, she does have good credit. I mean, I'm sure she'll make the loan payments. I don't know. Maybe a nurse is a nurse? This should be the last deal I do for Milt.

It is so hot in our house. Everybody is so crabby.

July 10, 1994

For as smart as Milt thinks he is, he sure does screw up a lot of his transactions. It seems like I am constantly fixing his mistakes. If he would just let me do my job, things would go much better, but he still insists on being the "go-between" for the borrowers. I am getting so sick of this. If he would just let me go directly to them, things would go much faster. Whatever. For all the work I do, I should be making $20,000 per transaction like Milt and his buddies do.

I asked Milton if Karen and I could come to his wedding reception. I told him that it would be fun to hang around with him and Milt. I actually just want to see what Milt looks like. He said that we could come. Then he kind of laughed. Something seems weird about this.

Karen is getting more and more annoyed that Milt calls at home in the evening all the time. Sorry Karen! I'm trying to make money over here for the family. Milt said he might be interested in being the financial backer for my music CD. Assuming I ever get it done.

July 12, 1994

I bought my first investment property yesterday. I bought it out of foreclosure for $25,000 with only 10 percent down. They even gave me a short term contract for deed. It's a three-bedroom, and I know its worth close to $45,000 – if I cut the grass and give it a paint job.

I know I can buy and sell houses better than Milt. I just know I can! Sometimes he can be such a moron. All I have to do is find a buyer. I'll be able to do that a lot better than Milt because I can size up a borrower quicker than Milt. I know the right questions to ask to find out what the buyer's credit is like before even running a credit report. I won't waste my time working with people who don't have a chance of qualifying. Watch out, Milt!

July 15, 1994

I mowed the lawn on my investment property. I can't believe I am the owner. I have two houses now – the home I live in and now an investment property. It's a big house, and I own it!

It's not a bad place either. Walking into it gives me the chills. It's old and kind of Victorian; it's completely empty. With the hardwood floors and nothing on the walls, it seems like an echo chamber. I should bring a piano in there sometime. I bet the acoustics would be great. I wish I could just keep it, but I can't. I'm trying to sell it to make the big bucks. Besides, I don't want to start making the monthly payments.

July 26, 1994

The "For Sale" ad I put in the paper to try to sell the investment property isn't working. I'm getting a bit nervous because so far, no one who responds to my ad can qualify for a loan. If I don't find a buyer soon, I'm going to have to start making payments. I don't have the extra money to do that for very long. I was over there last night and the neighbor guy told me that I shouldn't be around there at night. He said it's dangerous for a white guy like me to be in that neighborhood. Holy crap, I didn't know this area was that bad. He was probably exaggerating.

July 27, 1994

Karen, Timmy and I need to take a vacation. I don't spend enough time with my little Timmy. This morning he and I went to the bank. He fell down in the parking lot and cut his chin and there was blood everywhere. I felt awful. I got him all cleaned up when we got home. Now he's running around telling people that he fell down at the bank. "Faw down bank. Faw down bank." Thanks

Buddy. Maybe you could tell everybody that I stink at adult supervision. Sometimes I think I might need some adult supervision.

August 8, 1994

Milt called and told me that he is going to Los Angeles tomorrow to look at some commercial properties. I wish I could be doing what he's doing. I want to buy a building someday. Anyway, Milt told me to keep everything on track. He said that he was putting me in charge. At least he won't be calling me five million times a day! Maybe I'll finally get a chance to do my job.

August 11, 1994

Karen and I went to Milton's wedding reception. Milt wasn't there. Big surprise! Milt always tells me that he and Milton are best friends. Surely you show up at your best friend's wedding. Milton said that Milt got hung up in Atlanta on business. I don't know if I believe that. Things seem to get more confusing by the day. I don't think I want to meet Milt in person anymore.

August 19, 1994

A gift-wrapped box was dropped off by a courier today. It was a bottle of Sapphire Gin and a wad of cash — $500 to be exact. I called Milt, and he said it wasn't from him. He said that he'd love to get mail like that. I know it was him. It had to be. We talk on the phone all the time – he knows I like Sapphire Gin; and money.

September 6, 1994

I've been getting a lot of business from my old referral sources lately. The loans are closing and I'm making some awesome money.

A few weeks ago, Milt came through with a buyer for the investment property I'd been trying to sell. It closed today. The agreement was to split the profit with him, which was fine. Somehow, Milt convinced the buyer to pay $56,000 for the property. I thought it was only worth about $45,000. I never thought it would appraise for $56,000, but it was a staff appraiser from my office here who appraised it. So what do I know? I'm not an appraiser. I got my $10,000 out of it, and I originally thought I would only get four or five grand. I know it was a little unethical being the loan officer for the borrower who bought my house while I made a profit on the sale. But I didn't falsify or cook up any fake documents and she seemed to qualify just fine. At least she qualified according to the documents I received from Milt – some of them looked suspicious, but I decided not to ask questions. I like this idea of buying low and selling high, but I don't think I'll ever do it with Milt again.

October 15, 1994

Karen and I are looking to buy a bigger house in St. Paul. Timmy just turned two. We're thinking of having another kid. I found an old Victorian house over near the Governor's Mansion. It's not as prestigious as it sounds. It's listing for $149,000. Milt thinks I can negotiate down and get it for $120,000 – boy, he's just full of advice. It has a mother-in-law's apartment on the third floor and a very fancy formal dining room. I think we can get a home equity loan from our current house for the down payment on the new one. Then, once we move in, we could rent out the old house.

November 3, 1994

Today, my boss asked me if I am in business with a guy named Milt. I told him that a guy named Milt May sends me a lot of pre-quals and that, yes, we've had a half dozen or so of them close. I also told him that Milt helped me find a buyer for a property that I bought and sold. I asked if I was in trouble. My boss said that he wasn't sure. Then he said something that I cannot get out of my head. He said, "The appearance of impropriety is as bad as impropriety itself." What the hell is that supposed to mean? Am I in trouble or not?

You know what? I don't care if I am in trouble. Big deal. If I get fired, I can work anywhere.

Of the dozens of applications I've taken from Milt's referrals, I've only had about seven or eight of them actually close. That's enough. It has become way too weird working with Milt and his gang. He has borrowers showing up at closings with thousands of dollars in cash instead of cashier's checks. That's one of the biggest red flags in the world. If he doesn't want a bank to start scrutinizing his fudged up documents and files, he has to stop being so stupid.

He's been giving me a couple hundred bucks extra every once in a while for all my hard work. Whatever ... it's not worth it, and I don't need him. I'm not going to work with him ever again.

I think I'm going to talk to Jerry about working in the community-lending department at his bank. We've worked together before and he knows I'm good at what I do. It's closer to the new house in St. Paul. I need to get out of here.

If I ever get my CD done, I should just pursue that rock star career.

Chapter **3**

Climbing the Entrepreneurial Ladder

January 6, 1995

It's a new year! The new house is great, I love living in St. Paul, my new job is great and Jerry, my new boss, believes in me. I love the community-lending department here. It's such a relief to be out of that old place.

I'm glad that I finally convinced Jerry that I'm capable of originating low-income loans. I guess that banks not only want to look good by making loans to low-income folks, but they also want to make loans to minorities. I couldn't believe I had to prove to Jerry that I have a good track record of originating low-income and minority loans, even though I am not a minority. But I did it. I showed him my award from Norwest for originating the most Community Home Ownership Program loans in our branch through the third quarter of 1994. And 44 percent of them were minorities.

The other big obstacle to getting hired was that Jerry had heard from my old boss that there were some suspicious loans originated through me by a guy named Milt. I told Jerry that I knew Milt, and I had come to believe over the course of several months that he was a very suspicious character. I said that I'd told Milt that I wouldn't work with him anymore. Jerry seems satisfied with that. I didn't feel that I could tell Jerry everything.

Thank God I'm done with Milt and his gang. I really believe that if I had continued to work with him, I would have been fired. That's all I need, my reputation ruined only a couple years into the business.

Our new Victorian house is cool and everything, but I don't think I'd buy something that needs so much work ever again. Husbands and wives should not work on home repair projects together.

February 4, 1995

Jim, one of the processors from my old office, works here. At least I know someone. I was walking past his desk this morning and I heard him arguing with someone on the phone about not being able to close a loan in under a week. For some reason, I thought of Milt. When Jim hung up, just for the hell of it, I asked who he was talking to. He told me it was a real estate investor named John Johnson. I asked him what the guy's phone number was and, sure enough, it was the same as Milt's. I couldn't believe it. Well, actually, I can.

I wonder how many other loan officers in this city Milt has worked with. I wonder how many names Milt uses. Anyway, I brought Jim into Jerry's office and told them both that I thought this was the slippery guy I worked with before. I suggested that they cut any dealings with him right away, and they did. There's my good deed for the day.

February 19, 1995

Karen is mad that I've spent so much money making my CD. I keep telling her that it is coming along very well, and the songs we've recorded so far sound great. I'm sure I can sell it once it's done. She used to listen to me play and sing my songs on the piano all the time. Last week I wrote a song about how crappy things are between her and me. I play it all the time. She hasn't even commented on it. I guess I'm trying to bring up this topic by playing this song. She's not getting it. It would be just like her to not want to talk about it. Things are getting crappy between us. I just don't seem to be very happy anymore.

February 23, 1995

Dan, the staff appraiser from my old job, stopped by yesterday to see my new house here in St. Paul. He asked me if I had spoken to Milt lately and I told him I hadn't. I remember that Dan did a lot of the appraisals on Milt's deals. Dan told me that he and Milt had done several real estate deals together on the side, and Milt stiffed him on some of the profits. Profits? According to Dan, Milt said that if he continued to push him on trying to get his money, Milt would send his “thugs” after him. I can’t believe he used the word thugs. Anyhow, I am extremely happy that I don't work with Milt anymore. I told Dan to cut his losses and get away from Milt and his gang.

March 3, 1995

Now that I work exclusively in the community-lending department, I never originate any loans over about $70,000. Since commissions are based on the loan amounts, it is exceedingly difficult to make good money.

I've been toying with the idea of starting my own real-estate investment company. I've absorbed quite a bit of deal-structuring knowledge by doing loans for real estate investors. Maybe Milt was good for something after all.

This may not be a good time to venture out completely on my own, as Karen is pregnant again. I’m pretty confident I can make a real-estate investment company work. Milt made it work, and he mostly fumbled around and screwed it up. It shouldn’t be too hard to do better than Milt. I’ll just try to take it one step at a time.

June 15, 1995

I passed the real estate exam with flying colors. I am proud to say that I am now a licensed real estate agent, working with Wilmington-Guthrie, one of the largest real estate outfits in town. This training and experience will, no doubt, be incredibly valuable for me.

I know I am one of them now, but real estate agents are still a pain in the butt. Most of them don't seem to know much about the mortgage process, so I spend a great deal of time helping them figure out if their buyers qualify. It is amazing how few loan officers call on real estate agents. When I was a loan officer, I always avoided showing up at real estate offices because I assumed there were always hundreds of other loan officers roaming around in there, fighting for their business. I was a sales wuss.

I can't help but look for good deals on investment property. I do searches every couple days on the real estate listing database. I look for listings that fit the profile: three bedroom, 1,100 square feet on the market for over five months (or expired). I look mostly in the North Minneapolis area – mainly because while I was working on Milt's deals, I became familiar with the values in that neighborhood. Some of these margins are between fifteen to twenty-five thousand bucks. Someday I'm going to buy these houses.

July 10, 1995

Being a real estate agent is hard. Listings are so hard to get. There are a lot of resources here like the real estate listing database, phone lists and sales tools, but it seems like it takes too long to get established. I sometimes wonder if I should get back on the mortgage side. With another baby coming this fall, I have to make more money. There must be more money in the real estate investment business.

Even though I don't really like what I'm doing, I notice that I've been trying to be away from home as much as I can. I love being around Timmy, but there really doesn't seem to be anything between Karen and me. We don't argue, but we don't communicate either. How much longer can I take this?

September 25, 1995

A lot has happened over the last few months. My new real-estate investment endeavor is officially off the ground, and I am the sole shareholder, president and CEO of Neighborhood Redevelopment Corp. I bought and sold my first house and deposited nearly $20,000 in the bank! I knew I'd be good at this. My years of experience as a loan officer has put me in a perfect position for this type of business, as I can easily identify which interested buyers will qualify before I do a purchase agreement. I also use Milt's method of making a cash offer and then finding a buyer to buy the house from me before I close on my original sale. It's convenient having two closings on the same day — once with the person I'm buying from and then, almost simultaneously, with the person I'm selling to. I still can't believe this is legal, but the closer at the title company says it's fine. Besides, Milt used to do it all the time. I realize it sounds pretty stupid of me to base my legal decisions on what Milt did but I'm sure the title company wouldn't do it if it were actually illegal. I've been thinking of how nice it is that I haven't heard from Milt in almost a year.

The music on all ten songs is complete! I just need to do the vocals and put the back-up tracks down and then the CD is done. I can't wait for people to hear it.

November 11, 1995

Yup, it's another boy! We were pretty sure it would be because of the ultrasound, but you never know. Wee call him Mikey. Once again, I am having one of the best days of my life. You just can't plan it any better than this.

February 21, 1996

With two little boys in the house now, it's hard to get anything done. Note to self: Get an office somewhere outside the house! The potential to make money with my new company is phenomenal! I found a great low-income loan program at a local bank for potential buyers. It's perfect for someone who is used to being a renter. If you add up a rental deposit and the first month's rent, the buyers need less money for a down payment to buy the house than they would if they were going to rent an apartment. This program does however require that the buyer take a home buying class through a non-profit organization. I've met some of the people there and they seem to be very supportive of what I'm doing.

I never thought of it this way, but I guess they see what I do as helping people get into homes. I guess I am, but sometimes I feel a little guilty buying a house for such a dirt-cheap price and selling it to someone for the absolute top of its value. I shouldn't feel guilty though, because the bank does the appraisal and it's not like these buyers *have* to buy my houses. They could choose to buy a different house or buy the house I'm going to buy before I buy it.

May 5, 1996

My new office is awesome — no kids running around. But now I'm actually lonely. I should put something up on the walls so it doesn't echo so much when I'm on the phone. The piano is an excellent addition to the office. The reverb is pretty good in here.

I think Karen got used to me being at home for the past couple months. She seems irritated that I can't help out with the boys during the day anymore.

June 16, 1996

Mike is my first employee. He's funny. It's great having someone to talk to when we drive around looking at houses to buy. I've taught him how to screen buyers when they call. I've found that the best way to do this is to ask them how their credit is. If they say anything *other* than "perfect," ask them why they wouldn't say that it's "perfect."

I have a good solid pipeline of properties to sell. I always have at least three houses at a time. Next month it looks like we're going to have gross profits of over $60,000.

I found a house over in Stillwater that I'd like to buy. It's about a mile away from the state prison over there. Karen thinks it could be dangerous. Whatever. Anyhow, if I'm going to be making $60,000 a month, I think I can afford a mortgage payment on a $625,000 house. No need to live in poverty when I'm making this kind of money.

One of the best things about having an employee is that I now have someone to take to a company happy hour.

June 26, 1996

Why would anyone work for someone else? I just don't get it. They spend their whole day doing things to make money for someone besides themselves.

Take Mike, for example. He's a great kid and everything, but here's his job description: help me find houses for sale, work up purchase and sale reports, screen potential buyers, help the buyers through their loan process with the bank, and then come to the closing with me.

I get a 15 to 20 thousand dollar check per transaction, and I pay him a basic monthly salary. I make ten times more than he does. My risk is minimal. My overhead is only about $3,500 a month. I wonder how long it'll take him to catch on. Imagine how much money I'd make if I hired ten more employees.

July 1, 1996

This low-income, first time-homebuyer loan program is unbelievable. I've heard of flexible underwriting guidelines before but this is nuts.

Shendoah has absolutely no credit accounts on her credit report, and she doesn't have any non-traditional credit either. She does, however, have some collection accounts. Get this – Harvey, the loan officer at the bank, gave the rental verification to Shendoah to bring to her landlord so her landlord could fill it out.

That's crazy. The borrower isn't supposed to handle those types of loan documents. So, the only credit reference the bank has on Shendoah is her rental verification that shows a grand total of a two-month rental history. She's getting approved today. This is unheard of!

With all the loan programs I've come across, this one almost seems criminal because of the lenient guidelines. I would never lend *my* money to someone with these financial circumstances. If I hadn't seen the guidelines myself, I would have thought they were fraudulent. But, I'm not the underwriter or the loan officer so I don't handle any of the loan documents—ever.

I'm not the landlord, so I'm not fudging on the borrower's rental history. I'm not the appraiser so I'm not artificially inflating the price. I'm not the non-profit organization giving her the required home-buying classes.

She does have sufficient income to qualify based on the loan program guidelines, and she does have the required $1,000 to put up for her share of the closing costs. I am the seller; that's it. Oh yeah, and I'm making a lot of money.

July 9, 1996

I have to figure out what to do with the mortgage referrals I'm getting from my past loan customers. I think I'm going to start my own mortgage company. I'm pretty sure Marty from high school is in the mortgage or banking business. I should find him. I wonder if he'd run a mortgage company if I started one. Hmmmm. Maybe Mike could also be a loan officer. "Mayne Mortgage" has a nice ring to it.

July 24, 1996

The CD is done. It sounds great. Derrick and Mave did an excellent job producing it. I have to find a duplication place to make copies. I think I'll make a thousand copies and start an independent record label. If I do, I'll call it "Planet Earth Records."

August 13, 1996

Marty was the perfect choice to run Mayne Mortgage. He's funny and smart. I gave him 30 percent ownership. I told him he could set his salary at $4,000 a month as long as he can make the company generate enough revenue to support it.

We need to hire loan officers, and eventually a processor. It also helps that my real estate investment company can share the office and infuse capital during this start-up phase.

We are selling our home in St. Paul and will be moving the family to Hudson, Wisconsin. The "$600,000 house in Stillwater" idea didn't work. Somewhere along the line, I had a reality check and realized I don't need to go from a $160,000 house to three times that. Anyhow, it's only a thirty-minute drive from Hudson to my office in Minneapolis, but the drive won't be too bad in my new Benz.

The move will be good for Karen. Her family and friends live there. Maybe it'll give her something to do. Maybe we'll start getting along better. Man, I don't know where this marriage is going. How would I really know if I'm not in love anymore? I couldn't live without the boys but sometimes I wonder why I got married at all.

November 30, 1996

My CD release party was a success. I sold 23 copies. Just think if I actually toured and advertised.

Chapter **4**

A Lot Like Life

March 22, 1997

This year I have busier than ever. Man, do I ever feel like a suburbanite in the new house. We've got the two-story, four-bedroom house on the cul-de-sac. We've got the two kids, the big yard, the riding lawnmower, and the big gas grill on the wraparound deck in the back. We are now only about two miles from the in-laws. Wa-hoo!

Mayne Mortgage is taking up a lot of my time, but it is doing very well. We now have three loan officers, an administrative assistant, and one full-time processor. I haven't had much time to do the Neighborhood Redevelopment thing. Buying and selling houses is becoming exceedingly unpopular in the Twin Cities. They now call it flipping. I don't understand what's so wrong with buying a house at a low price and "flipping" it for a big profit when it sells. I don't think it's bad, per se. Whatever.

March 29, 1997

I'm not home very often anymore. Traffic is awful going through the Twin Cities to get to my office on the west side of Minneapolis. If I wait for the traffic to die down before I go home in the evening, I don't make it back until about 7:00. Karen gives me the silent treatment all the time now, so quite frankly, other than seeing the boys, there's really no reason for me to be at home. Karen and I are going on vacation to Spirit Mountain in Duluth next week. Maybe this will rekindle our marriage. Or maybe we'll realize we really aren't in love anymore. I hope Marty and Mike can keep things together at the office.

April 15, 1997

I got a call from someone who bought one of my houses last year and she said her roof leaked. I felt bad for her, but this makes me mad. On the real estate transfer disclosure statement, which was part of the purchase and sale documents, I indicated that the roof and the basement leaked. I did that on all my houses because I've never lived in any of them and I had no idea if the roof or the basement had ever leaked. I certainly wasn't going to say that the roofs and the basements have *never* leaked. I figured I'd just put it out there and if they wanted to look into it, we would do that right up front when they were signing the purchase agreement. Also, she signed my extra disclosure statement that I put together that said she had the right and duty to inspect the property. That was the same disclosure statement where I stated I was not her real estate agent and that I was doing this for a profit.

Anyhow, I told this lady that I'd send my handyman over there to take a look at it. She threatened to report me to that non-profit organization. Whatever, lady.

May 9, 1997

I moved out of my house last night. I asked Karen if she loved me, and she said she didn't know. Then she asked me the same question. I said I didn't think so. That pretty much says it all.

I'm sure it's going to be really hard for a while, but it's probably for the best. The mortgage company is continuing to grow, so I can afford to have an apartment in addition to paying for the family house. What's it going to be like, not seeing the boys? Oh, my God! Their births represent two of the best days of my life. Maybe we'll go to counseling and work it out.

June 1, 1997

The guy from the non-profit called me today and told me I needed to fix that lady's roof. I told him that maybe I'd help her out. I couldn't believe it when he said that he wasn't sure what they were going to have me do for this lady yet. What? What? *They* haven't decided what *I* am going to do yet? He said they did some research in the county records and found out that I made over $20,000 on that transaction and that I should give it back. Give it back? What a freak!

June 19, 1997

It is really hard being without my boys. I didn't think being separated would be this hard. We've worked out a schedule where the boys come and stay with me every other weekend. I know this sounds crazy, but I don't really know what to do with them when they're here. There's not much room in my one bedroom apartment. Brian gave me the name of his therapist.

June 28, 1997

A group of people, apparently organized by that non-profit company, stormed my office and disrupted business today. Understandably, it freaked out my employees when the non-profit zealots picketed with signs outside the office and chanting, "Don't buy a home, from Jerome." I'm trying to maintain a position of authority as boss over here. According to the protestors, I'm making too much money on the houses I sell to low-income buyers. Apparently, they don't realize that we all live in America. Wait until they find out that retail stores mark up their clothing by more than 50 percent!

The therapist thinks I did the right thing by leaving Karen. He said it'll take a while to adjust to the whole arrangement with the boys and that I'll be okay.

July 8, 1997

I've been seeing this therapist for about three weeks now. He thinks I have bi-polar disorder, which is the same thing as manic-depression. I've never thought of myself as depressed – manic, maybe. He had me see a psychiatrist who put me on a drug called Depakote. He said it won't work unless I stop drinking. I guess it would be an understatement right now if I said that I drink a lot. He thinks I should quit and go to AA or something. He says that I'm going around my emotions instead of experiencing them. It's harder to go through a mountain than to just walk around it. But he said life is hard and that ultimately, it will be better and satisfying if I put the work into it. I don't know what to do. I need to do something. I am going crazy. I looked in the mirror tonight and I don't know who was looking back. How long have I been this way?

October 3, 1997

Life has been very hard. I did the 90 meetings in 90 days in AA. Even after three months of sobriety there is still trouble in a lot of areas of my life. But, at least I think I'm starting to figure out who I am.

The non-profit zealots haven't given up yet. They are really starting to scare me. My lawyer and I had a meeting with them today. They are saying that I forced people to buy crappy houses. Just to get them off my back, I agreed to pay for home inspections for ten of the houses I bought and sold. I don't know what they think they're going to learn from a home inspection now. It's been a year to a year and a half since these people bought the houses.

December 15, 1997

I know that the separation was the right thing to do, but I'm not looking forward to my first Christmas without my boys. I've adjusted to seeing them every other weekend, but every other holiday is just going to kill me.

Work is much easier now that we've pretty much closed down operations on Neighborhood Redevelopment. Mayne Mortgage is quite profitable now that we have four originators. I'm excited about moving to the new office in Roseville next month. Finally, we'll be in a real office building and hopefully, with a better corporate image, we'll be able to attract some heavy-hitting loan officers from around town.

July 10, 1998

Mayne Mortgage is now up to 10 employees — well, nine after firing Eduardo for running off to Jamaica with that borrower's fiancée. He is a good friend and has been there for me a lot since I quit drinking. I hope we can continue to be friends. I've always thought that his style has been questionable. It will probably be best if he goes. I don't need any more trouble from non-profits or authorities. I don't think it would be good for the corporate image if I got sued for something stupid that Eduardo did. Worse yet, I wouldn't want to get into trouble with the Department of Commerce and have my mortgage license put in jeopardy.

It's hard to believe that just a few years ago I was sitting in an office all by myself hustling for business. Now I have a whole office full of people. I teach my sales staff how to drum up business and, more importantly, I make sure that everyone is happy and enjoys working here. We might open up a warehouse line next month. I think it would be smart to get a line in place and running smoothly before we bulk up on more staff next year. Marty is a godsend. He's good at math.

I started taking an improvisational comedy class. It's like theater, except we perform scenes where we make up all the lines on the spot. It usually turns out pretty funny. I've never done this kind of thing before. It's therapeutic. It actually seems like a stress-reliever after being at the office all the time and stressing out about my kids and wife. My teacher, Pamela, is extremely attractive. Maybe I should start dating again.

August 4, 1998

John died today at age 41. Heart attack — just like Dad. Good God, what's next? He is now the second of my brothers to die. This now makes me think quite a bit of my own mortality. His one-year-old little girl will never really know him. This is so sad.

August 23, 1998

Finally some good news. Mayne Mortgage is going to have a record in loan originations this month. At least it's something to brighten these dark skies of late.

It still amazes me that I work from about 8:00 in the morning until 3:00 in the afternoon. I see the employees bustling about when I leave. I know they are making money for themselves, but they're also making money for me. That still kills me. Why don't they just go out and start their own company?

Haven't heard from the non-profit zealots in a few months. That's also good news. They probably realized they were being ridiculous. Or is it just wishful thinking? Either way, it's nice that they've stopped.

August 27, 1998

I signed the final divorce papers today. It's not as shocking as I had anticipated. We have joint custody and all, but I'm paying a fortune in child support. We've either got to sell the house in Hudson or I'll have to move back there. It's not a bad house. It's really big for just me alone, but the boys are used to it and it's only about a mile from where Karen lives.

October 8, 1998

When I first started drinking again last month I was really scared. But I've found that it's really not a problem like it used to be. The fifteen months of sobriety was good for me. Looking back, I think that the reason I was drinking so much was that I was having such a hard time leaving my home and my boys. Now my life is going great. I'm loving my new friends in my improv class, and thanks to Marty, the mortgage company basically runs itself.

November 5, 1998

I wonder what it would be like to sell the mortgage company and just pursue improv and comedy. I really enjoy the improv. I'd like to get back into doing plays in a theater like I did in high school. For now though, everything is cool. I like the people I work with at the office. I don't know if I really want to sell something I've spent so much time and effort building and growing. Maybe someday. I still haven't done anything with my music CD either.

November 28, 1998

I can't believe how naïve people are – or maybe they're just stupid and lazy. I had to tell everyone to stop working with Kevin. Kevin's the shadiest real estate person I've ever met. He even rivals Milt. My God, I haven't thought of Milt in a while. Anyhow, it's plain and simple. Kevin lied to us.

He said that he's a lawyer. I called the Minnesota State Bar Association and they said they've never heard of him. He said that he attended the University of Minnesota law school. I called them and they said he never attended law school there. I don't really know why he told us that he was an attorney because he doesn't need to be one to buy and sell residential real estate.

Of all people in the office, I can't believe Brace, the good Christian, is mad at me for telling him to stop. Brace should understand that if this guy lied to us about something that is not material to him doing business with us, then how can we trust anything else he tells us? Besides, Kevin strictly works with foreclosures. There's something I don't trust about people who work with digging homeowners out of foreclosure and then selling the house back to them on a contract for deed.

December 4, 1998

I'm really starting to dig Pamela. I should be hesitant dating my improv instructor but I really like her. We've been hanging around each other a lot more lately. We always go to Rudolph's or the

Peanut Bar for cocktails after improv class. Even though everyone else from class is there, we always seem to sit by each other. I think she likes me. I don't know if she thinks we're just good friends or if she likes me like "that."

The loan officers are complaining again that business is slowing down because of the holidays. Whiners! What about working harder? I'm going to make everyone watch *Glenngarry Glenn Ross*. Then they'll see what hardcore sales are like.

I can't seem to get Charles to move a loan application along the process to close. He takes a loan application and then puts it on a stack. He must have about 15 applications on his desk. Hey, kid, how about getting those damn things closed? You'd think he'd want to make some money. I guess it's my job to help him with that. Patience. Patience.

December 16, 1998

I'm looking forward to Christmas because it's my turn to have the boys this year. Also, my comedy classes have become quite interesting. Pamela and I are "seeing each other." The other students don't know about it yet. It's kind of exciting to be covert about it.

Business is good, everyone's happy and we are all making lots of money. For the company Christmas party, I'm taking them to a fancy-shmancy restaurant and then to Pamela's holiday improv show. Good food. Good laughs. Good people.

Chapter 5

12/18, My 9/11

December 18, 1998

Oh, my God! I was out to lunch with my old buddy Koski today, bragging about how well my company is doing. He was the one who doubted me when I told him I was opening my own company. Anyway, my cell phone rang and it was Dianne, my assistant. She said there were two guys there at the office for a 12:30 p.m. appointment with me. It's not like me to miss appointments, and I was sure that I had nothing scheduled. It sounded fishy, and I thought that perhaps it could be those non-profit zealots again. Anyway, I asked her to take a name and number and I'd call them back to set something up.

Five minutes later, my cell phone rang again. The guy on the other end identified himself as Bob Canada with the FBI! The next thing he told me was that he was going to be taking me into custody today.

At first, a smile actually came across my face. I was sure that it was my neighbor, Jimmy. So I said, "Jimmyyyyyyy." Mr. Canada repeated what he had said initially. I listened carefully for any sign of chicanery in his voice ... none whatsoever. If this guy was faking it, he was good.

He asked me where I was, because he and his partner were going to come and pick me up. I asked him what this was about. He asked me if I wanted to do this the hard way. I didn't understand what was going on. So I asked him, "How do I really know that you are with the FBI?" In retrospect, that was a bad question because he then told me that he would turn on his car's lights and sirens if it would make me feel any better. I immediately told him that I was in the town of White Bear Lake. For my safety I asked if I could meet him at the police station there. He said that was fine but that I should wait in the parking lot and not go inside. Now it really began to sound fishy. I had Koski follow me there and hang around just in case they weren't really FBI. So, I hopped into my Benz and went to meet them.

An unmarked sedan with tinted windows wheeled into the White Bear Lake Police Department parking lot. Two men stepped out and said they were going to take me to FBI Headquarters, downtown Minneapolis. They had me turn around and put my hands up against the car. They searched me and asked if I had anything stupid on me, like a knife. All they found was my inhaler. I bet they don't find too many criminals toting asthma suppressants. They put me in cuffs and sat me in the backseat of their car.

Everything was going in slow motion. I wasn't quite sure how to sit in the backseat of a car while wearing handcuffs. You have to sort of shift to the left or right while putting your coupled hands opposite from the way you are leaning. It took me a few minutes to discover this listing technique so at first I sat on my hands and they twisted into the cold, tight metal clasps. My wrists still hurt tonight.

It was while I was being transported to FBI Headquarters that they explained that I was being charged with conspiracy to commit mail fraud, wire fraud and money laundering. I couldn't for the life of me think of what they were talking about. And they wouldn't give me any details. At first I thought maybe it was about Eduardo or some trouble one of my other loan officers got themselves into. What a great way to find out. For a fleeting moment, I thought it might have something to do with Milt. But I dismissed that quickly, as I hadn't spoken with him or his buddies in more than four years.

We turned off the busy downtown street and into an alley. That's when the sounds and bustle of the city went on mute. It felt like a Batman setting — skyscrapers were bordering this narrow little alley and thrusting up into the clouds, a garbage dumpster up ahead added to the setting. We pulled up to what looked a little bit like a loading dock. A man stepped up to the car. He was well-dressed. He wasn't wearing a nice suit like I was, but he certainly dressed sharper than Mr. Canada and his sidekick.

As we rode up the elevator, the well-dressed man told me that I was there because of my association with my buddy Milt and the rest of the gang. He wasn't mad at me. I guess he was just doing his job. I actually felt a bit relieved after hearing that all this was about Milt. It was at that point I knew I would eventually be able to explain this and that everything was going to be all right. I always knew there was something slippery about Milt and his gang and I told the well-dressed man that. He told me that I probably shouldn't talk anymore.

They took a picture of me holding a sign with my height, weight and birthday printed on it. It's amazing, they'd prepared the sign ahead of time, which means that they probably knew this morning that they were going to nab me today.

There also seems to be a real skill to fingerprinting. After they press your digit onto the ink pad, they have to roll your finger across a specific space on a piece of cardboard. As the "fingerprintee," you can't be too stiff, rigid or tense because the print will smudge. My "fingerprintor" and I went through three sheets of cardboard. Yeah, I was starting to get scared.

They put me in a room with chairs and a phone. It looked and smelled like a junior high school classroom. No expensive furniture here. I have no idea why the government would choose to skimp here. Anyhow, they said I could make some calls. I got a hold of Marty at the office. I explained to him what was going on, and he thought I was kidding. I told him that everything would be okay as soon as they came back into the room. I told him that I'd have a chance to explain everything. Marty seemed cool with that. I'm glad I told him about Milt last year. See, it's always good to tell your business partner about your past. Now Marty knows that I wasn't kidding around about my stories and suspicions of Milt. I asked Marty to meet with the copier guy, who was showing up at 2:00 p.m., if I wasn't back by then.

The well dressed-man came back in and put the cuffs back on. He closed them with my hands in front of my body instead of behind my back. Apparently, he was being kind because I guess they're not really supposed to do that.

He still didn't want to hear my explanations about my non-involvement with Milt. He said he was in a hurry because he wanted to get me in front of the U.S. Magistrate before he went home for the day. If your title is "Magistrate", I guess you can leave the office as early as you want.

Once in the Federal Courthouse, they brought me to a small holding area just outside the courtroom with several little jail cells. The well dressed-man put me into one of the cells and shut the cell door. At least he was nice enough to take the cuffs off while I waited in there.

I looked around this little jail cell and saw a stainless steel toilet and sink. I realized I was getting dizzy, so I sat down on a cold, stainless steel platform. I guess this was supposed to be the bed. It looked like a veterinarian's examination table. I didn't know what to do with myself. I didn't know what was going on with anything. I was afraid that the Magistrate might have gone home already. I suppose they could've kept me in there overnight.

Several hours later (I know it was only a few minutes but all this was progressing in slow motion) the guard or the bailiff or whoever he was brought me into the courtroom. I couldn't believe it when I saw Milton and his brother Rodney. My God, I hadn't seen any of those guys in years! They still looked the same. I wondered where Milt was or if he was getting in trouble for all this stuff too.

My name was called and I went up front and center. The United States Federal Magistrate was sitting in his perch behind the bench. It seemed as though he was 100 feet above me. When he looked down, his little old head eclipsed the United States Seal of Justice, on the wall behind him. He pointed his crooked finger at me and said something like, "Jerome Mayne, how do you plead to the fraud charges brought against you by the United States of America?"

I just about soiled myself. I have never been so intimidated in my entire life. I don't think I'll ever forget those words. There I was, still picking the basil out of my teeth from lunch. Now, just ninety minutes later, I was on the other side of a conflict with the United States of America. Most *countries* don't even like being in that position, let alone individual humans. So I've got that going for me.

I pled not guilty. Not as a strategic move or because I had it calculated that way, it's just that I'd seen it so many times in movies and on TV that it came out automatically. You hardly ever hear people on television say they are guilty right off the bat.

After I sat down they called up a guy named Brian Paar. Apparently, he was involved in this big conspiracy as well. He also pled not guilty. And when he spoke, I heard the voice I hadn't heard in years. Even though I'd never actually met Milt, I certainly knew his voice. Four and a half years ago, that voice called me ten to fifteen times a day. And every time, it identified itself as Milt. So now I know that the Milt on the phone is known by the authorities as Brian Paar.

Those hours were filled with moments I'll never forget.

A half hour later, this part was over. They let me out on what they called a signature bond. A $25,000 signature bond is a contract that says if you don't show up for your next court appearance, you owe them $25,000. That sounded easy enough because by the time there is another court appearance, I'll have explained this whole misunderstanding and that will be that.

I took a cab back to my car at the White Bear Lake Police Department's parking lot. The FBI isn't real keen on giving you a ride back to your car.

I got back to my office just as Marty was finishing up what should have been my meeting with the copier guy. I apologized to the salesman for missing the appointment. He seemed okay with that. I didn't say anything to Marty. I think he understood I needed to be alone. I'll talk to him about it tomorrow.

I went into my big corner office and shut the door. I looked out the window that leads to the inner office — the pit — and saw my loan officers screwing around. Chris threw a Nerf football at my window. I gave the office quarterback a smile as I shut my blinds.

I sat on my desk for a long time, looking at my file cabinet and my potted eucalyptus tree. I saw the projected closings for the month sitting on my desk. These guys were actually doing well for December.

I left the office early, again, and came home. I'm sure that in a few weeks I'll have a good laugh about this but right now, I don't know what I'm going to do. I'm sure I'll be able to straighten this whole thing out, but what if I can't? Will I lose my mortgage brokers license or get a huge fine? That would ruin me.

It's just so hard to believe that was I actually taken into custody today. Custody — like someone has custody of a child. Children need to be in the custody of a grown-up because they cannot always be trusted to make good decisions or act appropriately in society. I am not a child. I am a grown man, president of my own mortgage company and father of two young boys. Yet I was taken into custody today for the same reason that children need to be watched. For a few hours today, it was decided by my country that I needed to be kept away from society.

It's time to chill a couple of bottles of Chardonnay.

Chapter 6

Merry Christmas and a Happy New Year

December 19, 1998

When I woke up this morning, my house seemed more empty and quiet than it's ever been. At first, I had the sinking feeling that something terrible had happened the night before. Like in college when you drink too much, then wake up the next morning and your heart stops for just a second. You think you remember something stupid that you did the night before – but you're not sure. It's somewhere between the time your eyes open and the time you physically remove yourself from the bed that you start to realize that perhaps something awful did indeed happen. You begin to sort through memories trying to find the ones that save you from your fear. As your head clears, you settle in on reality. You sit there deflated, knowing that this awful thing might not get undone.

I've only felt that way a few other times in my life. There's of course, that time in college, then once when my father passed away, then the death of each of my brothers, then again when I left a five-year marriage. Now, I can add this morning to my list. Yesterday, the United States government charged me with conspiracy to commit mail fraud, wire fraud and money laundering. And I don't have the foggiest idea how I am going to straighten all this out.

I talked to Jerald, my attorney. He told me I should get an actual criminal defense lawyer. Jerald doesn't think I'll be able to just "straighten it out." I hope he's wrong. He's a business attorney, not a criminal defense attorney. Anyhow, he gave me the name of a guy in downtown Minneapolis. I called him and am going to meet with him next week.

I've been trying to piece together that whole eight to nine-month time period when I worked with Milt and his gang. I know I met him in March 1994. It's right here in my journal. I mean, I remember Milton and Rodney. And of course I remember Milt, or should I say – Brian Paar. But there is this other woman who was also indicted, Tamika. I don't really remember her. We'll just call her the fifth co-conspirator. I think I remember seeing her name on some of the loan documents.

Nonetheless, I'm pretty damn sure I didn't do anything wrong. Now that I've had some time to think about it, this thing really pisses me off. Okay, I shouldn't get too uptight about anything until I talk to this criminal defense attorney on Monday.

December 20, 1998

I called everybody in the family and told them what happened. I think I've convinced them that I really didn't do anything illegal. This whole thing is almost silly. It's not like I'm going to lose my mortgage company or anything. One of my brothers asked me if I was going to wind up with a felony on my record. That's ridiculous. You don't get a felony when you didn't do anything wrong. Then he said, "Usually the FBI doesn't yank you out of a restaurant, put you in cuffs, haul you downtown, fingerprint you, photograph you and charge you in federal court for fraud and money laundering if you didn't really do anything wrong". I guess that's what big brothers are for – to put you at ease.

December 21, 1998

First thing this morning I talked to Marty. He's very cool about it. It is fortunate that Marty and I go back so far — his mom was my kindergarten teacher. I've told him everything I can remember, and he agrees with me: they'll probably drop the whole thing once I explain my involvement – or lack thereof. We did agree that he should probably hold the brokers license for a while instead of me. We are both pretty sure that nothing will happen.

Just to be safe, I told him that we should probably be ready to change the name of the company too. I'm not sure how I should approach the guys in the office. I haven't known them as long as I've known Marty. It would financially devastate the company if I loose the big producers. I'll just have to trust that my authority as the boss and leader of the company will convince them that everything is fine, despite what the newspapers might say. Besides, I know they'll have a good time at our Christmas party.

December 22, 1998

I met with my criminal defense attorney for the first time this morning. I guess I can call him *my* attorney since it does look like we'll be working together. I told him the whole story. I think he believes me. He says that if what I am saying is true we probably won't get to trial. We'll probably plead out. I told him I'm not pleading to anything because I didn't do anything wrong. He said that we shouldn't get ahead of ourselves. He said that he has worked with this U.S. prosecutor before. The first thing he'll do is call the guy and ask what it is that he really wants with me. That made me feel a whole lot better. He knows the prosecutor!

Then we talked about money. He said that we should start off with 10 to 20 grand. Start off with! We're not even talking about going to trial. I told him that I just took out a home equity loan, but I used it to pay off some credit debt and to do some home improvements. I told him I could probably get five to 10 grand for him right now. He said that would be a good start and that we could discuss it again after the first of the year. My monthly bills almost come to 10 grand. I mean, I'll have it, but not if I want to pay my child support and mortgage payments on my rental property. Holy crap!

He told me not to talk to the press. The press? I hope there isn't any additional press at all. But, if there are going to be reports, I want to make sure they get it right. He said that if I ever have to take the stand, he wants the words that come out of my mouth to be the first words anyone ever hears from me about my involvement. I don't want this to be in the papers. They should wait until I can straighten this out. If they do put stuff in the papers about this, I want to be able to defend myself. I'm sure my attorney is right though. He's done this a lot more than I have.

I had to call my family again. They were able to help me out and lend me the 10 grand. It was hard to ask for. I thought, "I know it's a lot of money, but I'm good for it." Besides, it's family. I get the feeling that some of them don't believe that I did nothing wrong.

Nobody is really at the office this week, as Christmas is almost here. I haven't really been there much either. I've been here at home, making holiday preparations because it's my year to have the boys. It's important that it's special for them. Timmy is only three, and it's the first year that he'll really understand that Santa Claus brings presents. It's just going to be the three of us in this big house.

Even though the two little ones will be here, I think I'll still feel alone. I can't stop thinking about all this legal crap. I also can't seem to stop trying to convince people that I didn't do anything wrong. Why doesn't it seem like anyone believes me?

December 23, 1998

Today I told Karen about the arrest and the indictment. Man, is she glad we aren't married anymore. Yeah, whatever. I really think she thinks I was involved. She was there the whole time I worked with Milt back in 1994. She talked on the phone with him quite a bit when he'd call the house. She should know I wasn't really involved. I remember telling her all the time that I thought those guys were slippery. That's why I stopped working with them. I can't let that get me down. She'll see. Anyway, I've told her about it now, and that's that.

December 24, 1998

The cookies and milk are laid out for Santa. The boys are in bed. The tree looks good, all lit up and with lots of presents underneath. I have given myself the gift of two bottles of Chardonnay.

December 25, 1998

I brought the boys up to Mom's today. Everyone was glad to see them. I felt like some family members were avoiding me. They acted like they're not sure if they even know me anymore. It's me! I'm the same guy. I did, however, come home with a check for 10 grand. That's going to be a huge help.

It was hard to bring the boys back to Karen this afternoon. I felt alone when they were here and now it's even worse. I am trying so hard not to let this thing beat me, mentally. I've pushed through tougher things before. Chin up. Forward march!

December 29, 1998

No one is scheduled to be in the office this week, so I've been calling everybody to talk to them, one on one. They've been good enough to stop in for a few hours when I asked them to. They all seem to believe in me. It is hard to tell though, with some of the newer ones.

December 30, 1998

We had our big office holiday dinner last night. Afterwards, I took them all to the improv show. They had fun and it was good to see Pamela. We got a good deal on our tickets because she owns half of the improv company. And now that we're seeing each other... She has proven to be such a good friend. I don't really know how awesome she will think I am when I tell her about all this legal crap. I'll just have to risk it. I don't want to get something going with her, just to have her find out later that I've been indicted for fraud. That would be unfair. This is so embarrassing.

January 4, 1999

I met with my attorney again today. I signed a representation agreement and also gave him 15 grand. He said that was a good first payment. Then he wanted to talk about property I could sell.

I couldn't believe it! Sell my investment property for this stupid legal fight, that isn't even my battle. I tried to tell him that I wasn't involved in any conspiracy — a plan to commit fraud or to launder money. He said it was fine that I felt that way. He also told me that it didn't really matter if I did or didn't do it, the only thing that matters is what can be proven. He said that he talked to the prosecutor and the prosecutor told him that he's, "got me" and that all the other defendants are saying that I knew what was going on the whole time. What?! He also said he has documentary evidence that I was "in business" with them.

I don't know what the hell he's talking about! Milt, his buddies and their buyers gave me documents and I turned the documents in. This is unbelievable. What do they want from me? Why are they trying to pull me into this? They've got the slippery people. Why can't they just leave me alone?

January 5, 1999

I received a letter from one of our lenders this morning. They are canceling the broker contract with us. They say that they heard about the indictment of "Jerome Mayne, one of Mayne Mortgage's officers." That's just great.

The crime had nothing to do with Mayne Mortgage. So working with Milt four and a half years ago has affected my business today. This really pisses me off.

I told Marty that I think we should sue the lender. They can't cancel a broker contract just because someone has been *accused* of something. I don't know if we can really sue them, but they're definitely going to hear from me.

That's just fine if they don't want any more of our business. They're the ones who are going to look stupid when this whole thing blows over.

January 6, 1999

I finally told Pamela the whole story. I wish I had told her sooner. She is awesome. She listened, supported me, and really gave me confidence. She's only known me for a few months but she said she thought I was a strong, confident man. I guess that's the only me she knows.

I put my Christmas decorations away tonight. Just for the fun of it, I wrote a note to myself and put it in one of the decoration boxes so I'll find it next year. It says, "Aren't you glad your legal troubles are over with?" I really hope I get to open that box next Christmas.

Chapter 7

Realizing the Elusive Truth

January 20, 1999

Things are going from bad to worse. Ever since the indictment, Marty and I have received more letters from lenders and investors telling us they are canceling our broker agreements. This is crazy. I haven't been found guilty by a jury, nor have I pled guilty. Not only that, but I have been *accused* of a crime that took place over four years ago, which was two years before I started this company. Innocent until proven guilty, right! I feel bad for Marty, because none of this has anything to do with him. It now seems pretty clear that we're going to have to change the name of the company to something else. And Marty is going to have to put the license for the new company in his name. I was hoping it wouldn't have to come to this.

My employees are acting weird around here. I mean, I understand but... Damn! I am so mad! I'm sure they're acting weird because obviously they can tell that I'm not myself. I used to spend my whole day making sure people were happy and enjoyed their jobs. Now all I do is sit in my office, worrying about what everyone thinks of me.

I've got my improv class tonight. I'm glad I started these classes a few months ago. It's like comic relief from my daily nightmares. It's also good to see Pamela. We've been seeing each other outside of class more and more. I hate to bring her into all this stuff, but I'm glad I told her everything that's going on. I'm *so* glad she didn't freak! I feel pretty lucky to have her right now – someone who doesn't judge me. She's also trying to get me to do stand-up comedy. What could it hurt?

January 25, 1999

I had my first real "work" day at my attorney's office. I agreed to get them another 10 grand in a month or so. They said that'd be okay since I was going to be helping them so much preparing the case. That'll be $25,000 just to prove I wasn't involved in this conspiracy. Thank God I'm still getting my salary.

The U.S. prosecutor's office produced about 12 boxes of documents. They've got my personnel file from Norwest Mortgage and dozens of loans I worked on. They also had my bank personal records going back to 1994. How creepy.

It felt sort of good rolling up my sleeves and going through these boxes. It's like I can finally put together some proof. It's a daunting task because not only do I have thousands of documents to organize, categorize and index, but I also have to prove that I *didn't* know what was going on. Isn't it impossible to prove a negative? My two years as a litigation paralegal are going to come in handy now.

January 27, 1999

My attorney asked the prosecutor if we could cooperate, and I could tell them everything I know. The prosecutor said they really didn't want my information because they know I didn't know enough to really help them with anything. What!? I thought a conspiracy meant that a group of people had a criminal plan. If that were the case, wouldn't I know the plan? And if I didn't know the plan, how could I be part of a conspiracy?

The more I go through these documents the angrier I get. I figured out what tipped off the investigation at Norwest. It was a string of first-payment defaults. So Milt, or Brian Paar, didn't make sure these bogus borrowers made their payments. How stupid! I told my attorney that if I'd been involved in this plan, I'd have made sure there weren't any first payment, second payment, third payment or any payment defaults. Anybody in the mortgage business would know this. My attorney told me that it would not be a very good defense to say that I would have done a better job at the crime. He's got a point there.

I'm starting to get the feeling that I'm not going to be able to explain my way out of this. My attorney said that if I go to trial and lose, I could get over seven years in federal prison. That is inconceivable! Seven years away from my boys – from my life – from everything – in PRISON — me?! I couldn't do that. Maybe a couple months. No, not even a couple months. I'm not going to prison at all. I DIDN'T DO IT!

I have my psychiatrist appointment tomorrow. In addition to the Depakote and Wellbutrin I take for the bi-polar disorder, I am going to ask him about Prozac for the depression.

February 2, 1999

Well, what do you know? Marty told me today that he and Bob, the new manager we just hired, are going to go across the street and start their own mortgage company. I just about spit.

I thought he was going to stick with me through this. He said that most of the other loan officers were going to go with him and Bob. I was speechless. I told him to have a nice time starting from scratch because all the closed loans and all the files in progress are corporate assets and therefore 70 percent mine.

I know I can't close over thirty files in the next two months by myself – especially with all this legal crap. But I'll be damned if I'm going to give these files away. So he said that he's going to make me an offer to purchase the assets. At least I could have some money to operate until this thing blows over. What a crappy thing to do – my business partner and childhood friend concocts a plan to split, while week after week I'm at my attorney's office putting together a case to try to prove that I wasn't involved in this stupid thing. I'm the one who gave him his 30 percent ownership!

February 10, 1999

My attorney told me that one of the defendants cut a deal and pled guilty yesterday. It was that woman I didn't know. That kind of freaks me out. I wonder what she said about me. I can't imagine what she'd say since I didn't know her.

I talked to Pamela about all this. She always listens and is very cool. She really is keeping me grounded. We decided to be just friends, which I suppose is fine with me. I decided to give stand-up a try. I have my debut open stage next week.

February 19, 1999

Well, I got taken to the cleaners. I sold the assets of the company to Marty today, but all I got was $20,000 and my laptop. Wow, I got to keep my own laptop! Oh wait, I almost forgot: I got to keep the remaining $97,000 office lease obligation, because I personally guaranteed it. But I still got my laptop! There goes my income. There goes my perfect credit. I don't know how I'm going to pay my child support. Well, at least I can give my attorney that other 10 grand. Perfect!

February 23, 1999

It's pouring rain. Today I got served with a civil suit by those non-profit zealots who picketed my office last year; that pathetic group of home buyers who bought houses from me when I had my real-estate investment company in 1995 and 1996. They said they were wronged because I made too much profit on the houses I sold them. And apparently, I somehow tricked them into buying the houses. What about the disclosures that everyone signed, where I told them that I was doing this for a profit? And that I didn't represent them in any way? What about the disclosure that said they had the right and the duty to inspect the property? What about the arbitration agreements? I get the distinct impression that the non-profit had an attorney bring this lawsuit because they read about Jerome Mayne, the big bad criminal, in the newspaper. They want $250,000. I don't know where they think I'm hiding my millions. My criminal defense attorney said that he cannot defend me in that civil lawsuit for free, but they would ask for a continuance until this criminal suit is over. "Calling all idiots! Step right up and sue Jerome Mayne!"

February 28, 1999

Pamela and I went back to my office today to pick up a few remaining personal things. I hadn't been there in over a week.

It was hard to get off the elevator and walk that long, familiar hallway to the front door of my office. I had walked down this hallway hundreds of times before. It wasn't until today that I realized I had been taking this hallway for granted. It is an excellent hallway.

I noticed the superb workmanship of the wallpaper hangers. The edges lined up perfectly. The design and the simple color scheme could set one up for a very productive day.

I finally got to the door. It was a nice door. It looked the same as it had for the past year or so, with the "Mayne Mortgage" sign still proudly displayed just to its right. I remember how much effort went into the design of that sign. It was backlit and made of dark green marble. That's right — Brian made it.

I knew I wasn't going to walk into an office bustling with commerce. I knew I wouldn't feel the pride and warmth of the quality people I'd hired over the years. I wouldn't get to help them feel good about their jobs today or teach them something new. Pamela squeezed my hand.

Walking in was just like the roller coaster of emotions you go through when you return to your old childhood home. You can feel the place. The smells help. You subconsciously feel the innocence of the child you once were. But then you look to the dining room and your memory plays the scene with you sitting at the table and your parents shouting and screaming at each other. Poof! The happy thought is gone.

I didn't think my office had its own smell, but it did. It hit the olfactory area in my head with a snap.

It immediately caused a feeling of pride and accomplishment. But as soon as my brain had a chance to process the goings-on associated with this smell, I deflated.

I was surprised to see that Diane and Charles were still there! Apparently some of our lenders hadn't heard about how much of a criminal I am, and had yet to cancel their broker agreements with us. Charles and Diane told me they weren't going to leave until someone came to take the art off the walls, and that they were definitely not going to work for Marty. That was an unexpected boost.

I feel like I've abandoned them. I know Diane can take care of herself. She's been in this business for 15 years, she'll find something soon. But what about Charles? He knows about my legal issues, yet he appears so oblivious to this reality. While I was there, he was feverishly making copies, shuffling papers from one file to another, faxing documents – he barely had time to look up and say hello. If I didn't know better I'd have thought he was clearing conditions on a loan that was closing in the next ten minutes. I felt so awful. He was like a puppy who shows up at the same tree every day to learn new tricks from his owner. Except one day, the owner stops showing up. The pup waits and waits and waits until someone takes the art off the walls. It's over, kiddo. Go home. I've got nothing for you. In fact, I wanted to tell him to run. Run as far and as fast as you can – and don't tell anyone you ever worked with Jerome Mayne. You have a whole career ahead of you. You don't have to carry my bag. God speed, young man.

I grabbed a couple files and the brass letter opener that I got as a gift when I incorporated my first company. I said my quick good-byes, then Pamela and I left.

March 12, 1999

I feel so bad for the two boys, Tim and Mikey. When they come over, all I do is sit around and stare out the window or at the TV. I don't feel like doing anything. At least when I stare at the TV, they think we're doing something together. I need to be a better father.

Money is so damn tight. My attorney told me why he believes me: it's because I don't have any money. He told me that usually the people who have money are the people who "did it." Everybody's a comic. He also said that this case is not looking any better or getting any easier.

March 20, 1999

I'm starting to get tired. The only things I care about anymore are my improv classes, stand-up comedy, spending time with the boys, and Pamela. Even though she and I planned on just being friends, it's clear now that it's more. I know it's stupid on both our parts with so much unknown. What a crappy time to fall in love.

March 30, 1999

The pretrial keeps moving along. Since I don't have an office in the Twin Cities anymore, I'm going to move back to Minneapolis. I need to be closer to my attorney's office. I think my rental application for the apartment made it in just in time — before all my creditors reported to the bureaus.

I've got the income from my investment properties, but I need money to live on. I can't both live and make the payments on the rental properties. I have come to the conclusion that no matter what happens in this criminal law suit, I will be losing my properties and my cars.

My attorney said that the prosecutor will continue to produce documentation, a little bit at a time. He said this is how it works. They'll hold on to the most damning documentation as long as they can. It's sort of like a poker game, I guess. I hate poker. What could they possibly have on me?

April 7, 1999

The trip to the Chicago Improv Festival was so good for me. It was really hard to come back. I was able to forget about all these problems for the whole weekend. It was good talking to the others in my performance troupe. I can say that they are my friends now. They are the ones who don't judge me. Most of my other friends seem to have dropped me. So it's Pamela and these four people.

Pamela officially told me that she wants to be more than friends. She knows everything. She knows what kind of person I am. She knows about all the potential outcomes of this whole lawsuit. I asked her why she wants to do this. And for some reason it made perfect sense when she said, "You can't choose who you fall in love with."

April 10, 1999

The prosecutor called a meeting with my attorney and me today. He told us that just to be fair he had to let us know that there have been death threats made by some defendants against some of the other defendants. He wouldn't say whether or not it was against me. Then he said that I shouldn't worry because the federal prosecutor's office pursues these actions very seriously. Pursues them? Great! So they'll definitely *find* my killer.

I've been thinking about asking Pamela to move in with me. What am I doing?

April 14, 1999

This morning the prosecution said they wanted to talk to me and maybe offer me a cooperation deal. I thought they said I didn't know anything. Why, suddenly, do they think I can help them? It sounds fishy and kind of risky. Here's the deal: I tell them everything I know and then plead guilty to all the charges. I would probably not get any prison time. "Probably". Hmm, should I trust the prosecutor?

My attorney said I shouldn't be nervous about pleading guilty to all the charges, because there's a special request that the prosecutor makes to the judge. They make a motion to drastically deviate from the sentencing guidelines. For instance, instead of seven years for money laundering, you get probation or something. He said you almost never get prison time when you do this. The scary part is that the judge can decline the prosecutor's special request. And since I would have already pleaded guilty to all the charges, I could be stuck with the maximum sentence for all these crimes. Hmm, should I trust my attorney?

This could be my big break, but I have to be cautious. Pamela is keeping me grounded, but I can tell she's excited. My attorney said that when the prosecution says they want to offer you a deal, as a professional courtesy between prosecution and defense, they stick by it.

"Professional courtesy." I sometimes forget that this is just a job to them. It's my life that they are being professional and courteous about. I suppose it's better than being hacks – lousy, unprofessional, foul-mannered morons.

I bet they're at home right now living it up, planning vacations with their wives and kids. That's the kind of thing you do if the federal government isn't suing you. They probably drove home this evening, got stuck in traffic while thinking about whether or not the Timberwolves will return to the playoffs this year. And maybe they'll go and see a game or two if the T-Wolves stay in it long enough.

My attorney is probably thinking about how well his business is doing. And how it will continue to do well as long as the accuser keeps accusing people, and the accused people need his help; ideas and methods to undertake the impossible task of proving that they're *not* guilty.

The prosecutor: he has a government job so he's not part of this whole free-market thing, {i.e., work real hard, get a ton of clients, win a bunch of cases, build a reputation and make a ton of money}. The prosecutor probably makes the same amount no matter what happens. Does he get a bonus if he wins? That would be awful if the U.S. Attorney's office is on a "salary plus commission" pay plan. They get another 10 grand every time they put ten accused citizens away. Hey, and if you win more cases than anyone else in the office, you get a T-shirt at the Christmas party that says, "I AM CAPTAIN MORON" and then on the back it says, "But I get to bring my wife and kids to Wally World".

So what do you do for a living? I'm a federal prosecutor. How about you? Oh, how quirky, I'm a criminal defense attorney. How about those Timberwolves? Want another cocktail?

Anyhow, back to this deal my attorney and the prosecutor are being so nice to each other about. I guess a prosecutor doesn't bring up the deal unless they are really ready to deal.

Pamela is excited. I know I shouldn't get too excited, but I can't help it. Excited isn't the right word. Nervously optimistic.

I've got to get busy and make a list of all the things I know that they don't know which could help them. Anything. Anything. Think. Think!

April 15, 1999

First of all, I can't believe my attorney didn't show up on time. I just sat there, by myself, waiting in the lobby at the U.S. Attorney's office. I was sitting there thinking that this really might be the meeting that gets me out of this mess. I knew I shouldn't have gotten my hopes up. The prosecutor is such a wuss that he couldn't come out and address me in person. He had to have the receptionist come out and tell me that I should call my attorney because things have changed. Yeah, I'll say they changed. My attorney said that he didn't know until this morning that they offered Milton a deal last night. Of course they did. He knows more!

My attorney finally came over to the prosecutor's office. At least he chewed out the prosecutor. I could overhear some of it. I heard my attorney say that in all his years, he's never had a prosecutor back out of a deal when talks have come this far. Thank God the nicey-nice between the two of them is gone. Maybe my attorney will get tough now.

I feel so defeated. I really thought this was my chance. That's two out of the five of the co-defendants who've now cut a deal. My attorney said that they really want Milt. Great, now that they've got him, why don't they just let me go?

May 4, 1999

I like my new pad. I've never lived in a warehouse apartment before. With the comedy club just down the street, it's much safer to stumble two blocks home than to drive all the way to Wisconsin – drunk.

May 15, 1999

I went to a temporary employment agency today and filled out an application. They said that they couldn't work with me because I have pending civil and criminal lawsuits. I should have lied on the application.

My days are lame. I really don't have much to do. I don't have the energy to go through those documents at my attorney's office anymore. I'm living off my rental property income, but I'm getting way behind on the payments. Almost every night I go to the open stage for stand-up or I go to an improv class. I am training to be an improv teacher now. That's cool. I seem to be spending a lot of time drinking after the classes or the open stages. I know I'm not supposed to drink while I'm on this medication, but I guess I don't know what it's hurting. How could my life be any worse?

May 26, 1999

Rodney pled guilty today. He didn't get a deal or anything. He pled guilty to lesser charges and has to take whatever the federal sentencing guidelines say. Now it's just me and Brian Paar (It's still really hard not to call him Milt). My attorney said I really should think about pleading out. He joked that it probably would be malpractice if he didn't at least advise me to plead to it. Real funny. He said I could still probably keep it to a maximum of 36 months. I don't think I could handle more than a year or so.

June 19, 1999

The prosecution showed their cards today. They weren't bluffing. This morning they produced documentation showing a trail of $10,000 going from Milt to me in 1994. That was the money from that investment property I bought and sold; the one where Milt helped me find a buyer and we split the money when it sold. I've been running around telling everyone that Milt is a shady conman; a criminal sleaze-ball. Well, this documentation doesn't make me look very good. It actually does put me in business with Milt.

July 8, 1999

My attorney called me this afternoon and told me that Milt was going to fold. This is bad news for me. If I don't cut a deal, I would be the odd man out – the last one out of the five co-conspirators. This would put me in the spotlight; make me the sole focus with a jury. He also said that the $25,000 I've given them so far doesn't cover a long drawn-out trial and at this point, that's what it would be.

I told Pamela that I think I might have to plead guilty because I don't have the money to fight it anymore and even if I had the money, I'd probably lose. I told her that I'll probably get about three years. Hey, it's better than seven. She somehow knew this was coming.

I just feel so beaten down. I don't have the mental strength to fight this anymore. And let's face it – there's no way I'd win. I can't lie to myself or anyone else anymore. I may not have known exactly what was going on, but I knew. I knew plenty. I was involved with a group of people who set out to defraud my employer. Without my involvement, my employer would not have lost money.

Seven months ago I had never even had a traffic ticket. And now I'm trying to decide what I would like better – three or seven years in federal prison.

Chapter **8**

Hurry Up and Wait

July 28, 1999

The past six months have been the most trying time of my life. It's been such a long fight. It's almost a relief that I've made the decision to plead guilty. Seven months ago I had a big corner office on the fifth floor of a beautiful office building, half a dozen loan officers, a photo copier, two processors, a business partner, dozens of lenders, respect in the mortgage community, a $10,000 monthly salary, five investment properties, one home on a cul-de-sac, a Mercedes Benz, a Jeep Grand Cherokee, perfect credit, a huge potential for growth, direction, and self-esteem.

But now, when I stop and think about it, I can't believe how far I've dropped and lowered the bar.

When I was first indicted I actually thought I was going to explain my way out of this – truly believing that I didn't do anything wrong. Now I've agreed to plead guilty to mail and wire fraud conspiracy charges, and accept up to thirty-six months in federal prison; along with a couple hundred thousand dollars in restitution.

Just this month I received default notices from three of my five investment properties. And since I can't sell, rent, or make the payments on my home in Hudson, I'm going to lose that too. At least I have enough income from two of my remaining investment properties so I can live in this apartment.

I have a hearing in family court next month to lower my child support payments. I feel terrible about not being able to support my kids the way I used to, but I just don't have the money.

I'd been waiting for the bank to come and repossess my Mercedes since I hadn't been able to make payments on it since February. I got sick of looking out my window for the repo-man so I called the bank and asked if I could just turn it in somewhere. They politely told me that they simply don't have a procedure for that and that there was really no place I could bring it to just drop it off. I guess they have a system – borrower doesn't make payments, repo-man tracks down the banks asset, repo-man waits for the borrower to fall asleep, repo-man confiscates the vehicle, repo-man's company puts it up for auction and pays the bank for a portion of the sale. I guess it makes sense since the bank isn't in the business of selling cars. I did manage to get the name and number of the repo-company they use. I called that company and made an arrangement that they would let me know when they were going to come and take the bank's car.

So they called me today and I turned over the vehicle. I didn't even have to sign any papers. The guy just drove off. Fair enough – I was the one who didn't make the payments.

August 3, 1999

My brother, who has his one-man mortgage broker shop at his home, agreed to expand his outfit and get a real office. He only agreed to do it if I help him run it as a consultant – a business consultant only. At least it'll be something to keep me busy, and I really need the money. I promised him that I wouldn't originate or process any loans. And I won't go running around telling everybody I work for him, so his reputation won't get ruined. Diane and Charles, from my old company, have agreed to work for my brother's company as long as I'm there. What did I do to deserve this loyalty? I must have done something right.

Thank God I'm still busy every night. I'm either in an improv class, training to be an improv comedy instructor or doing stand-up. Pamela is a great improv instructor and a great supporter for me in my stand-up. It helps to laugh and make people laugh. It's a good form of therapy. It's also convenient that these nightly activities take place in a bar where I can drink until it's time to go to bed. I know it's self-destructive, but I probably won't be drinking much longer.

I wish I knew what was going to happen. Exactly how long will my sentence be? Where will I be going to prison? When will I go? What will it be like? This not knowing is killing me. It's so weird telling people that I'm going to be going to prison. Most of them don't believe me. I guess I don't look the part. Most people don't know anyone who went to prison, so they just go off the impressions they have from the movies.

Hell, I can't even connect the dots. The line just doesn't seem to go there. But I am going to prison. Me.

Pamela still wants to stick with me through all this. I gave her the option of hitting the bricks, but she said she's in love and can't change that. Wow.

August 24, 1999

Today I pled guilty in federal court – in front of the United States of America. My attorney said I couldn't say that I had a "really strong feeling" that things weren't right. I had to tell of specific things I did as part of the conspiracy; specific things I knew about. He also said that I couldn't even hint at the notion that I wasn't involved, or else I could get more prison time for not accepting responsibility. He also said that if the judge didn't believe that I believed that I did it, they could throw the whole deal out and make me go to trial.

So I did what I was supposed to do. I told about the time that I neglected to re-verify the employment of a borrower after I had knowledge that she changed jobs before closing. Then I stretched the truth and said that I knew about all the phony documents, referring to the documents I discovered during pre-trial. I also told the truth about the cashiers checks I received as a result of the sale of the property I sold with Milt. The cashiers checks that were intentionally written to two friends of mine – for the purpose of hiding the fact that I, the loan officer, received money from the sale.

And the judge bought it. I never thought I would feel a sense of relief that a federal judge would accept *my* guilty plea so that I could go to prison without a hassle.

I'm now officially a convict and a criminal. People probably will think of me as a sneaky, untrustworthy, "watch your money or I'll steal it" kind of person. In the eyes of everyone but a few close friends and some of my family, I was guilty from moment I was arrested. Do the newspapers lie? Does the FBI and the Federal Prosecutor's Office spend years investigating someone who didn't do anything wrong? The public doesn't think so. Innocent until proven guilty? For all intents and purposes it never really mattered. I keep going through a cycle of anger, hopelessness and guilt.

I am at a place now that I honestly don't know what I knew when this was going on back in 1994. I think I had myself convinced that I was completely innocent. I didn't want to think of myself as a bad guy. I'm not a bad guy, am I?

Part of me thought that I was actually more ethical than some of the people I worked with. I always thought fraud was committed when people had a plan and bilked millions out of unsuspecting citizens. Or, when they crafted a scheme where they wound up with millions of dollars from a bank or an investment company. I thought it was the stuff you read about in the papers. I wonder if any of them felt the way I feel now. I never thought of myself as a liar or a cheater or a stealer. I know I'm not. I am definitely at the lowest point I can ever remember in my life.

Pamela and I decided that she should move in with me. Her 2 ½-year-old son and my two boys will stay with us every other weekend. It'll be crowded in the one bedroom apartment, but it'll be kind of like a sleepover. It should also help fight the loneliness.

Pamela and I decided to take a road trip to L.A. before I have to go away. Sentencing is in a couple weeks and I still don't know for exactly how long or to what prison I'll be going. Even though I'm scared to death, I just want to get this thing over with.

August 25, 1999

This suspense is killing me. Where? When? How long? Has my sentence already started? It sure feels like it has.

I'm at the point now where I don't want to make any new friends because, well, what's the point? I had to stop working with my brother's mortgage company. I just can't bring myself to do anything related to the mortgage business. I hate it now.

And now for something positive: I finished somewhere in the top fifteen in the Amateur Twin Cities Funniest Person Contest. I didn't make the top ten, but top fifteen isn't bad out of 125 contestants. I think I lost because a 75-year-old woman fell down and hit her head on the brick wall on her way off stage. Nice strategy grandma – an intentional pratt fall. Just my luck, I was up next. Oh well, it *was* funny.

August 26, 1999

Tonight at the comedy club there was a guy I'd never seen before – another amateur comic like me. He did jokes about being in federal prison. I thought someone might have put him up to it as a joke on me. Afterwards, I asked him if it was true. He said he just got out a few months ago. He'd been at the federal prison in Duluth, Minnesota, for three years and then was transferred to the federal prison in Yankton, South Dakota, to finish his final two. Wow! This sounds crazy, but it felt so good talking to this ex-convict.

He told me all about both prisons. He said that when I go to sentencing I should make a request to go to the prison in Yankton. I guess the judge might honor my request. Apparently, Duluth is okay, but pretty damn cold in the winter. He did five years for drug dealing. I guess both places consist of about 90 percent drug-related offenders. What? I thought I was going to a white-collar prison, but apparently they don't exist. Now I'm really freaked out. He told me about a book I could get online called *Down Time.* I guess it's like a "going to federal prison" handbook. It was written by an enterprising ex-convict.

September 2, 1999

I just got back from the annual canoe trip with the guys from high school. My ex-business partner, Marty, was there. I should still be mad at him for not sticking with me throughout all this.

I'd like to say that I wouldn't have split on him if the roles were reversed, but who knows? I mean seriously, what if he'd stayed with me? He'd now have a business partner who pled guilty in federal court. I have to admit now that I really don't blame him. He has a wife and two kids. Where would he be now? Unemployed? Shunned by the industry? Guilty by association? He would be the guy who was in business with the criminal. I wanted to stay mad, but I just couldn't.

Tomorrow Pamela and I leave on our road trip to L.A. We are going for two weeks. I wonder if the feds somehow know about this. I wonder if they think I'm going to skip off to Mexico.

September 3, 1999

Pamela and I are having a blast. Tonight we're staying in Rapid City, South Dakota. It's right by Mt. Rushmore. Since we started out in

Minneapolis, we went right through Yankton, South Dakota, where that one prison is. I couldn't resist stopping by and seeing the place.

We marched right up to the front building. I guess this is where you go when you report for prison. It's also the visitors entrance. A guard came out and asked if he could help us. He looked a little bit like Jesse Ventura but with a more defined walrus mustache, and his head didn't shake. He seemed very pleasant. I think he assumed I was there to visit someone. As I was poking my head around, I told him that I might be going there in a month or so. I told him that I just pled guilty to fraud and I was awaiting sentencing.

His disposition changed immediately when I told him I was a criminal. It was like he could now look down upon me as a lower life form. I asked him a few questions about some of the buildings on the compound. His answers were very short, and he didn't really want to make direct eye contact with me or Pamela anymore. It was very uncomfortable.

We got the hell out of there in a hurry. For a second there, I thought he was going to haul me inside. Think about it. I am guilty. I said so.

The place looked okay. As far as the aesthetics, I think I could go there. I've been to Duluth before. Not the prison, but the city is cold even in the middle of summer with that wind coming off Lake Superior.

I guess I'll just have to wait and see what the judge says. Anyway, I gotta try to quit thinking about all this and enjoy my final vacation.

September 15, 1999

We got back from California yesterday. I didn't want to come back. I mean, of course I was coming back, but God, this is horrible. The nightmare continues. My attorney told me to carefully choose a few people to ask to write character letters to the judge. People like former associates, friends and family. He doesn't want these people to say that I'm a great guy and that there's no way I could've committed these crimes. Because if they do, the letters won't have a whole lot of credibility. I mean seriously, I already said I did it. Anyhow, I guess this helps the judge get a feel for what kind of person I am – other than a criminal. It feels like I have now lost all dignity.

My attorney also informed me that he is turning my civil fraud case back over to me, the one with the big non-profit organization, since this criminal matter is basically over. Yeah, it's over for him. I can't afford an attorney so I'll just have to defend myself. What can it hurt? Maybe it'll take my mind off this other crap.

Chapter 9

Condemnation

September 30, 1999

Sentencing day. It's real. It's real. I have to keep telling myself that. It's real.

For the past several months I've known this, but somewhere in the back of my head I've been hoping that this was someone else's life; because it just can't be mine.

Today at the federal building in downtown St. Paul, certain things seemed to go in slow motion. If it was a movie, the screenplay would look something like this:

FADE IN

INT. FEDERAL COURTHOUSE (1999) - DAY

A dimly lit hallway of a typical government building.

Expensive, shiny marble walls and several long, thick marble columns hold up the ceiling.

JEROME MAYNE, a man in his early thirties, casually dressed, black shoes freshly shined, waits in line at the metal detector that guards the entrance and occupants of this high-level security building.

With its tall ceilings and cold stone walls, this ominous foyer doubles as an echo chamber.

Mayne's body language is that of a man who might turn and bolt from this line at any minute or maybe even pull a gun and take a hostage.

His left eye develops a tick.

In tow is Mayne's girlfriend, his brother, his mother and his best friend from college.

Mayne's posse makes it through the metal detector check-point without incident.

SLOW MOTION

Mayne places his watch and pocket change into a plastic basket, then hands it to a slow and unsmiling, gray-haired security guard named LENNY, who has never seen a gym in his life.

Mayne passes through the upright, manila-colored metal detector.

A BEEPING sound, accompanied by a FLASHING RED BEACON, erupts inside this echo chamber.

Mayne spins 180. Hands slightly outstretched from his sides. Knees bent, he instinctively takes a steadying position and locks onto the eyes of Lenny who has suddenly come to life.

The other bystanders at this checkpoint turn towards the sound of this security breach.

END SLOW MOTION

Somewhere, a SWAT team deploys.

A second security guard named ROY, thick of neck and brow, appears from behind a wide marble pillar. He carefully approaches Mayne toting a two-foot, jet black, hand-held metal detector wand, which also could double as a beating stick. Every breath in the room is held.

ROY
Please turn around
and place your arms
directly out from
your sides, sir!

Mayne complies. Roy slowly passes the wand across every inch of Mayne's body. A bead of sweat trickles from Roy's crew-cut. The detector detects nothing.

Lenny approaches and accepts the wand as Roy relays it back to him.

ROY
I am now going to
do a hand search!
Please stand still
For approximately
thirty to forty-
five seconds, sir!

Mayne's shoulder muscles begin to atrophy as he continues to hold his arms out-stretched from his sides. The physical body search takes place with the guard standing behind Mayne. It is slow and deliberate.

While patting down Mayne's chest, Roy suddenly lurches backwards, two giant steps. Lenny ducks for cover behind the pillar.

ROY
Please remove the
item from the inside

(MORE)

ROY (CONT'D)
pocket of your sport coat and set it on the floor directly in front of you!

With his right hand, Mayne slowly reaches inside his sport coat and into his left breast pocket. He slowly removes a four-inch-long, aluminum cylinder, mostly encased in white plastic.

Several GASPS are vomited about the crowd.

ROY
I'm only going to say this one more time - please place the contraband on the floor in front of you, and step back!

Mayne complies.

Lenny peers out from behind the pillar. Roy, apparently the weapons expert and future member of the bomb squad, approaches Mayne's mysterious object.

He slowly stoops to visually examine it then musters up enough courage to pick it up.

Roy un-holsters his two-way radio.

ROY
(into the transmitter)
Stand down, blue team! Stand down. It's ahh asthma inhaler.

MAYNE
Oh for God's sake.

The Roy slowly turns to his partner and gives him a nod of suspicion but belief.

The guards reluctantly give the "all clear" to the crowd and a collective sigh of relief reverberates about the space.

Mayne grabs his asthma weapon, his watch and his pocket change from this rent-a-government-agent. He turns and traverses – half-cold, heel-toe, heavy-feet echo – to the elevator bay.

FADE OUT.

TO BE CONTINUED

Okay, so my imagination was very active today. Either that or I'm going crazy. The latter is likely. I'm just trying to keep my sense of humor.

This is serious and real. People use the phrase "slapped with a sentence." Today I got slapped with a twenty-one-month sentence. The sentence range was between twenty-one and twenty-four months, but the judge said he'd go with the twenty-one. And for the first time since I knew of this prosecutor's existence, he didn't object. What a sweetheart. Geez, I hate that guy.

I learned that the judge received dozens of supportive character letters from business associates, former employees, friends and family, on my behalf. I cannot find the words to describe how those letters made me feel. The judge commented that he rarely receives this kind of an outpouring. Yeah, I bet he thinks I'm a real great guy.

I did get my first choice of prisons – Yankton, South Dakota. I should get my reporting papers in a few weeks. Since I'm a white-collar criminal, I'm not dangerous enough to have Con-air fly me over there or get escorted by the federal marshals. I get to find my own ride. Thank God I've got Pamela. I can't imagine asking my mom for a *ride* to prison.

After the sentence-slapping, the judge asked me if I had anything to say. I stood and told him that there was nothing more powerful and intimidating than the federal justice system. And I assured him that I would do everything in my power to avoid being in this situation ever again. I made no apologies. I prepared that little speech ahead of time. No one seemed impressed and sentence didn't change.

After the final gavel hit, I looked at my four guests in the pews behind me. My mom, one of my brothers, my old friend Brian, and Pamela cried.

So did I.

October 15, 1999

After much ado about nothing, the plaintiff's attorney for my civil case, the one that has nothing to do with this criminal trial, agreed to drop me personally from the suit. He agreed to take a default judgment against my old investment corporation instead.

He thinks he'll be able to collect $250,000 judgment from the State Emergency Real Estate Relief Fund. I don't think he knows it yet, but he's wrong. If I read the statute correctly, he won't be able to collect from the fund. I believe a civil fraud judgment against an "individual" must be presented in order to collect, and my old real-estate investment company is not an individual.

I understand that the Department of Commerce usually looks into default judgments very carefully. They can even force the plaintiffs to prove that fraud actually occurred. Good luck. Who's committing the fraud here? Okay, that's over. I've just got to let it go.

October 16, 1999

I got my reporting papers in the mail today. I am to report to the federal prison at Yankton, South Dakota, on November 4th between the hours of 12:00 p.m. and 4:00 p.m. Pamela will bring me. I think we are going to need each other in those final hours.

November 4, 1999

I went to Karen's house last night and said good-bye to Tim and Mikey. They won't miss me as much since they're only used to seeing me every other weekend. I have been preparing them for the past two months. I thought I explained it to them in a way that a 3-and a 6-year-old would understand.

It's difficult for young children to understand the concept of a year in time. It's hard for Mikey, at three years old, to understand what a week is for that matter. However, they both know that Santa Claus comes once a year. So, I told them that I would be gone for "two Santa Clauses".

They seemed fine with it all. But when I gave them that one last squeeze, I lost it. They knew. You can't *really* pull the wool over a child's eyes.

I used my shaving razor for the last time this morning. I realized that subconsciously, I've been extremely judicious about using my remaining shampoo, soap and deodorant. I guess I didn't want to use it all up and then have to go and buy a whole new bottle of shampoo, which would then just sit there for two years. So apparently I now deplore the waste of toiletries? How strange. I wonder if this is like preparing to die.

It's time to get in the car. Pamela is acting like she's holding up well. She's not. I'm not. But I gotta go. This is it. I did a bad thing and I'm going to prison today.

I'm all ready to go. I have nothing to pack. Nothing to bring. I'm not even allowed to bring this journal. Goodbye.

Chapter 10

Dear Sweetheart

November 5, 1999

Dear Pamela,

I'm really here. I'm actually writing to you from the federal prison in Yankton, South Dakota. It's only been about 18 hours since I last saw you. I miss you so much. It's so hard to believe that I'm really here. In prison. Prison!

It's quite a bit different than waking up next to you. I'm guessing you didn't sleep too well, in our bed, without me either. I just can't believe it! Me. I'm actually in prison. By the time you get this letter, I'll have made it through about four nights. Hopefully, I'll have slept by then. You too.

As I lay in my bed on the plastic mattress and the plastic pillow, I can't help thinking about the events that led me here. I never would've thought that five years ago, when I met Milt, or should I say Brian Paar, I would wind up getting convicted of conspiracy to commit mail and wire fraud and receive a 21-month prison sentence. I keep thinking about everything: getting arrested, spending 25 grand in attorney's fees, losing my company, house, cars, business associates, friends, and finally spending my first night in prison.

Another prisoner here was nice enough to lend me this paper, his pencil, this envelope and a stamp so I could write you this letter.

After you and my mom dropped me off, the guards took me to a small concrete building called R & D, which stands for Receiving and Discharge. They did the same things the FBI and the U.S. marshals did when I was arrested 11 months ago. They took my finger-prints, and they also took my picture for my prison ID. They took my clothes and my bi-polar medication I had in my pocket. This letter is probably going to reach you before you get the box with my clothes and shoes they are sending. Anyhow, they are sending you everything that walked through the gate with me yesterday — except me — so don't be alarmed.

They gave me a pair of underwear and a set of socks. I don't know what they were made out of, but I wouldn't know where to buy something that crappy. They also gave me a tan jumpsuit and faded blue, floppy cloth slippers to wear until I went to the laundry department. I think the slippers and the jump suit were hand-me-downs.

They have all my personal info from my pre-sentence investigation, so they knew I was on Depakote, Wellbutrin and Paxil. Thank God they know I need that stuff. When they caught me with the pills in my pocket, I was afraid they were going to think I was trying to smuggle drugs into the place. I guess I was. Anyhow, I had to wait an hour and a half in a cold little room until the prison psychiatrist came to see me.

He finally arrived. He had my pills and said I could go to the medical department once a day and they would give me my dose. He also said that we would meet in a couple days and decide if I still needed them. Maybe I'm crazy, but I've been on that medication for quite a while. I don't think now is the time to go off medicine that keeps me from feeling anxious and depressed. He wasn't surprised when he saw me shake and when I told him I was scared. I really tried to hold it together when I was with him because I don't know what they do with you if you freak out. He said I would adjust to this place. I can't wait until I adjust.

After meeting with the psychiatrist, they handed me a document, opened the door and pointed me to the laundry department which was about 200 yards away. It was surreal. There I was, a former finance professional, father of two, walking across the compound, in prison, all by myself. There were dozens of other prisoners walking and standing around. I was waiting for them to shout or point and laugh or take bets on how long I would last in this place. A couple of them glanced over at me as I walked by but no one really seemed to care. By the way, no one here wears the orange jump suits. What a relief. They all wear either white T-shirts or button-up khaki shirts and khaki pants and dark or black boots. I didn't see anyone wearing a gray jumpsuit with floppy slippers except me.

Somehow, about halfway to the laundry department I got turned around and lost focus of the nondescript door on the nondescript building to which I was pointed. The document they handed me in R & D was not a map. I assume they frown on maps around here. I mean, it's not like they pointed me to a door labeled "Laundry." There was no "Laundry" sign. Trust me, I checked.

I tried to act like I knew where I was going. I tried to match the walking speed of the other criminals because I'm sure they all knew where they were going. I walked up to several doors and stood there just looking around. It is impossible to look like you know what you're doing when you walk up to four different doors without entering. I was afraid to open them. God only knows what was going on behind those doors. Finally, I saw a guy walk out of a door carrying a pair of pants. I don't know why he was carrying a pair of pants. I mean, he was wearing pants. Anyhow, there it was. I struck laundry.

The laundry department was hot and humid and full of other prisoners. It reeked of what I hoped was soap. Prisoners were working in there. It turns out everyone here in the prison has a job. I don't know what my job will be yet. I gave my document to some guy, an inmate, because that was his job and he asked for it. Some guy told me take off my jumpsuit while he went to find me a pair of khaki pants. Never in my entire life has someone said to me, "Hey, take off that jumpsuit," let alone a prisoner. Anyhow, I took it off and suddenly missed my hand-me-down gray, jumpsuit. I have to tell you honey, it was quite uncomfortable standing in a room with ten prisoners wearing only stupid underwear and crappy socks. I wasn't embarrassed about the underwear or the socks.

Anyhow, I left there with four pairs of khaki pants, four khaki shirts, four white t-shirts, four pairs of white socks, one set of gym shorts and a half-worn-out pair of black work boots. They put an iron-on patch on all of my cloths. They all read "MAYNE 08657-041." The guy told me that this is my name and number. Really? So I thanked Einstein. Well at least I won't forget my number.

They also gave me my bed-clothes, which consisted of two off-white sheets (I think they were supposed to be white), one black wool blanket, one gray bedspread and one off-white pillow case. I also got two towels and a washcloth. Everything just barely fit into two large, white, nylon fishnet laundry bags.

The guy handed back my document and told me my next destination was Kingsbury. That's the building where I am housed, but I didn't know it at the time. He didn't open the door and point to Kingsbury. I guess I was just afraid to ask. I left the laundry department, lugging my two big sacks of supplies over both shoulders. It dawned on me at that point that I was not wearing or carrying anything that belonged to me three hours prior.

I walked to the middle of the compound so I could get a good look at all the buildings. None of them were labeled "Kingsbury." At that point I didn't care if I looked like I fit in or not. I set the bags down because they were just too heavy and it was all I could do to keep from having a total break-down.

As I stood there, center compound, I had a chance to get a 360-degree view. I let myself take it all in. The sun was shining. Green grass. Colorful fall trees. Birds. It was the sights and smells of nature and the outdoors; except for the fact that dozens of prisoners were walking and sitting around. Some were just sitting on benches, smoking. Some of them were raking leaves and mowing the lawn.

Then I saw a beautiful rose garden – then another and another. From where I stood, I counted four. Maybe it was just odd to me because I was new, but prisoners were working in them! Some with greasy hair, unshaven faces, tattoo-covered arms – and not all of them looked unhappy. These hardened criminals were tending to flowers. It turns out that there's a college horticulture degree program in here.

Just then one of the prisoners walked up to me and asked, "Where'd you come from?" This was my first social conversation with a real prisoner. His name-tag read "Mathews." I didn't catch his number but it doesn't matter. I didn't know what he meant when he asked me where I came from.

Obviously, I came from the laundry department, but I didn't want to insult the guy. I found out later that many of the prisoners in here have been transferred in from other institutions around the country. So when someone new shows up they want to know if you've seen one of their old buddies in Lompoc or Duluth or wherever you might have been. I know this sounds stupid, but when he asked where I came from, all I could say was that you and my mom just dropped me off.

About eight other prisoners, who were standing around, started laughing. Hey, at least they weren't mad! I guess when you "self-surrender" like I did it's not as cool as getting hauled in here wearing cuffs and chains. So that was the price I had to pay for directions to Kingsbury.

Once I got to my housing unit, one of the guards showed me to my room in the basement. They call the rooms "cells" and their roommates, they call "cellmates." It's not a cell like you might think. There aren't any bars, so I don't get it. But I think I should start using the prison vernacular so I fit in.

First of all, the smell was horrendous. It still is. I guess it's just one of those things I'll get used to. At least now I have gotten past the gagging part.

There are three bunk beds in my "cell." I got a top bunk. Apparently, the lower bunk is a coveted spot taken by those with seniority.

I made it through the first night without anything really bad happening. I know because I was awake for the whole thing. All of my cell-mates were sleeping. The snoring was out of this world. It sounded like one of those carwash vacuums sucking air through two big slabs of raw prime rib. Multiply that by five criminals. You thought *I* snored.

The guard poked his head in and shined a flashlight on each one of us three times last night in order to count us. Apparently, they'll be doing that every night. I pretended like I was sleeping. I was a little scared because I didn't know if I was going to get caught "pretending to sleep." I mean, technically, that's tricking the guards. I'm pretty sure you're not supposed to trick the guards around here.

My roommates are actually pretty cool. They all told me not to worry and that I'd be just fine. There was that elusive "just fine" again.

I asked all of them what they were in prison for. Mike and Cliff are in for having crystal meth labs (not the same case), Jamal sold crack to a DEA agent (not on purpose), Mac got caught with a suitcase full of cocaine on a train from New Mexico to Los Angeles (it was his). And then there was Doc (he loaned me the letter writing supplies).

Doc looks and acts like the warmest, most gentle physician you might find in a family clinic – except for the fact that he wasn't wearing a white doctor's coat. Anyhow, he used to be an ER doctor but he got himself hooked on morphine. I guess he got caught writing prescriptions to himself, which is a crime. He was sentenced to six months of probation (no prison time) but also had the other standard felony restrictions, like not being able to vote or have a fire-arm. He wound up in prison because one day he realized he had an old rifle – a Musket – in his attic. He wasn't supposed to have a gun, so he turned it in to his probation officer. Since "having a gun" was a violation of his probation, they sent him here to prison. That sounds crazy, doesn't it? He doesn't seem like a liar, but who knows?

I went to the chow hall for breakfast this morning. I really screwed up. I went through the line with my tray and then had to find a place to sit down. I didn't see any of my cellmates so I just went and sat at an empty table. One of the other criminals came over to me right away and told me to move because I was sitting at the guard's table. How was I supposed to know the seating arrangements?

It seems like the guys watch out for each other around here. Everything right now is scary. I don't know what I'm supposed to be doing. I'm sure I'll figure it out.

I have to go to orientation tomorrow in the chapel. I'm really looking forward to it. Maybe I'll start to understand how things work around here. They gave me a handbook to read before the meeting. It lists things that are not allowed. If you do anything on the bad list, you can get sent to the "hole." Anyhow, the first thing on the list is "No Murder." That really freaked me out, so I asked one of my cellmates how many murders happen around here. He said, "none."

I didn't think it was such a stupid question. I mean, it was in the rule book. Why would we need to be told to refrain from murder unless it happened from time to time?

I am going to write a letter to Karen, asking her about the boys coming to visit. I know you guys don't really get along but if she agrees, maybe you or my mom can bring them out sometime. The visiting room is very nice, with an area for kids and their dads to read books and play with toys (we don't have to talk on the telephone through a glass window). I just don't know what I'll do if I can't see them for 21 months. My mom said she would pay my ex-wife for collect calls that I make to them.

I have enclosed the forms you need to fill out so you can get approved to come and visit. If you send them right back, maybe you can come next weekend? I know this is hard on you, and like we talked about before, I don't have any expectations about your coming here to see me a lot. I mean, it would be great and everything but I don't expect it.

I will try to give you a call as soon as I get phone privileges. It'll be collect, but you can use the income from my duplex to offset the costs. Oh, and if there is any left over, could you send $50 to $75 to the prison? It has to be in a money order from the post office. Put my inmate number on the check, 08657-041, and they'll put it in my account. I get to go to the commissary store once a week and buy things like tennis shoes, pens, stamps and stuff like that.

I just have to tell you once again how sorry I am that you are going through all this. I know you said you are in love and that's just how it is. But I want you to know that if it becomes too much for you, I understand. This isn't fair for you. You're not the one who committed the crime, I was. So you shouldn't have to go through prison.

It's strange how I was the one who messed up but everyone close to me has to go through this too.

Write soon.

Love, Jerome

Chapter 11

Letters from the Inside

November 18, 1999

Dear Sweetheart,

My job isn't so bad. In fact, it's a little too easy. I sweep four flights of concrete stairs, scrub problem steps with a dirty little bristle brush, and then I mop. Some days it only takes me about 45 minutes. Then I have to find something to do to look busy or else I could get kicked off this job. They could put me on grounds keeping duty. If that happens, I'll be out shoveling snow this winter. I'm learning how to sweep and mop real slow.

A kid named Chad got released last week. He's been in here for about five months for selling meth. He was supposed to have about six months of probation or as they sometimes call it, "supervised release." He just left last week but now he's back in! I guess he failed a UA (that's prison talk and it means they found trace amounts of THC in his urine analysis). Anyhow, he's only 18! He seems to like it here. Well, he must, because here he is. He knew exactly what would land him back in here. He went out and did it anyway. I wonder if his mom is as proud of him as my mom is of me.

About a year and a half ago, at this hour, I left my office and went to meet Koski for lunch. By 12:30 in the afternoon, my life, our lives, had changed forever. Actually it had changed four and a half years prior, when I met the Miltons.

I think back and try to figure out what could I have seen; what I could have done differently? I am convinced that there was no way for me to know that Milt and his gang had crimes planned – at first. But there were so many things in the ensuing months that were huge red flags that I ignored or justified.

One of my cellmates, a drug dealer, said that his type of crime is more honorable because with drug dealing, no one is tricked out of money. His crime involves activity where both the buyer and the seller know how much money is changing hands, and both parties are getting value for their money. He calls it a victimless crime. He said that in white-collar crime, one of the parties has no idea that money is changing hands at all, and the ignorant party, the victim, is getting no value for his money.

In the drug world, I can think of a lot of victims, direct and incidental. But it did make me think.

Well, that's all I have to say today. Write or come visit me. You know where I am.

November 22, 1999

Traveler,

Greetings once again from Yankton!

Thanks for coming to visit me. Two weekends in a row! Wow, you must really like me. It's hard to believe that you drive over five and a half hours – 325 miles each way to come here from Minneapolis.

I still haven't been able to reach the boys. Karen won't accept the collect calls. I don't understand this because my mom said she'd pay for them. We're just going to have to send her some cash up front.

I don't get it. This is so frustrating. I have no control over anything in my life. It doesn't seem fair that I lose the boys for this whole time – or that they lose me. They didn't do anything wrong.

November 30, 1999

Lovely,

My birthday came and went yesterday. Thirty-three years old, Wahoo! What a way to spend my Jesus year.

I saw the *Minneapolis Star Tribune* here in the library today - maybe you saw it too in your paper at home. For a while, I was glad I'm able to see the hometown paper in here, but I wish I wouldn't have seen it today.

That creep of an attorney who represented those non-profit zealots wound up getting a story in the paper about the civil lawsuit against me. Gee, maybe it's because he's a columnist for the damn paper. It was such a bunch of crap! We settled the case! If I wouldn't have been on my way to prison I would have fought him all the way. And I would have won! Why did he settle? Because after I showed him all the disclosures the buyers signed and the arbitration agreements and all the other disclosures, he realized that he had a bogus case. Why else would he have dropped it? And so of course the story in the paper refers to me as "Jerome Mayne, currently in federal prison for a fraud conviction." So now the belief is "Of course, he did it. He pled guilty in the federal criminal case and he basically pled guilty in this civil case. It must be because he's guilty." Now people think I was involved in a smorgasbord of fraudulent activity. Oh yeah, everything I've ever done, my whole life, has just been riddled with fraud. Well just look: I *am* serving time in federal prison. I must have been involved in criminal activity since the day I was born. So now, even if some people thought, "Well, maybe he made some mistakes when he was younger," they certainly don't think that now. Is this how it's going to be for the rest of my life? Maybe I shouldn't have pled guilty.

Sorry, sweetheart. I just feel so helpless. I'll talk to you this weekend – I gotta go.

December 2, 1999

Pamela,

I was standing in a big group of inmates after mail call this evening. We were all waiting at the door of our housing facility to be released to the chow hall. A guy next to me was hollering about a letter that was returned to him because he put the wrong zip-code on it. He looked over his shoulder just as I was glancing over at him and his erroneously zipcoded envelope. Then, he turned and squared off at me. He hollered at me to mind my own business. I remembered something I saw or heard in one of those movies, *Shawshank Redemption* or *Escape From Alcatraz* or something. I can't remember, but the rule is: Don't ever back down or look scared. I know what you're thinking – I should've just walked away. But you have to understand, I just couldn't. So I squared off right back at him, stared into his face and waited just as long as I could, and I said, "I *am* minding my own business." Then he pointed to the corner and told me to stand over there. So far, I was keeping my composure. Then, adhering to the rule, I stood my ground and in the toughest, white-boy bravado I could muster, I said, "I'm fine right here." He looked around as if to check for cops (that's what they call the guards here) and then, he walked away. It worked! I couldn't believe it. The only other fight I've ever won was with a jammed Xerox copier. But now, I basically won my first prison fight.

I don't expect you to be proud, but I may have just made things easier for myself in here.

December 3, 1999

Sweetheart,

You say that you're interested in sticking with me through all this. I've gotten to know you pretty well over the past year. You've stuck with me so far. But I have to tell you, I've been hearing a lot of talk from guys in here who've been dumped. I'd say that there are very few who have had their wives or girlfriends stick with them for even a few months. Why would we be different from the norm? Odds are we're not. I don't mean to sound so negative but when you think about it, the odds are not in our favor.

December 4. 1999

Pamela,

Sorry about the letter yesterday. I was really having a bad day. You know what? When I have a bad day, there's really nothing to look forward to. The staff or the guards are not going to cut me slack. They're not going to say, "Okay, you can just sit in your room today. There, there young man. Everything's going to be okay. Can I get you anything? Hey, if you just need to talk, we're here for you. Glass of water? Chocolate milk?"

This self-pity is hard to fight.

December 6, 1999

Pamela,

You'll be happy to hear I won't be getting into any more prison fights. I heard of a beating that took place last night. Some guy told the cops that his roommates had a cell phone hidden in the wall in their cell. I guess they really did have one. They must have smuggled it in through the visiting room – I don't know. I guess they had hollowed out a space in the brick wall behind the bulletin board in their cell.

Apparently the snitch was beaten so badly that he defecated in his pants – not to mention the talk of the blood and broken bones. They took him to the hospital, and I guess he lived. The tough guys have been removed from the facility. Rumor has it that they won't be back.

But seriously, that's the only fight I've heard about in here. There really aren't many fights. I don't want you to worry.

I'm looking forward to seeing you this weekend. I know you won't get this until next Tuesday and you'll have already seen me. So, thanks for coming.

December 9, 1999

Lovely,

I'm going to be moving to a different housing unit called Durand. All of the people in Durand are in a program called DAP. It's that Drug and Alcohol Program I was telling you about. That psychiatrist said that I qualify for the program because during pre-trial I disclosed that I was taking my bi-polar medication while drinking almost every night. They said that that indicates alcohol abuse. I say it indicates I was preparing for prison. Okay, I admit it was alcohol abuse and I know it's a problem.

So now I get to go to a class four days a week from 8:00 a.m. until 11:30 a.m. with about twenty five other people. I don't know what I am going to get out of it, but I guess it can't hurt. Besides, it is something to do to pass the time. The program lasts nine months so I'll definitely have time to complete it.

Here's the great news: If I complete the program I'll get up to a year off my sentence and I'll get to serve out the final six months of my sentence in a halfway house (some people only get to serve out the final month or so).

For me, the halfway house will probably be somewhere in Minneapolis. I heard that a halfway house isn't as tough as prison. You get to wear your own clothes and get released to go to a job during the day! I bet that'll feel sort of like freedom. Isn't that cool?

I still don't know exactly how long my sentence will be. I mean, it is twenty-one months, but I'll get time off for good behavior. It's hard to calculate how much time one gets off for being good.

I'm just going to assume that my sentence will be the full twenty-one months – that's fifteen months here in South Dakota and six months at a halfway house in Minneapolis. Worst-case scenario, I'll get out of here on February 4, 2001, to go to the halfway house. And then, if I complete DAP, I'll go to the halfway house for six months and be completely done by August 4, 2001. That seems like forever. I hope there's a better-case scenario.

I've only been here for a month. It already seems like it's been forever. It's going to be twenty more of those months until I get to walk around in my own clothes a free man; twenty more months until we can do something as simple as go to dinner; twenty more months until I can go to the store and buy a jacket or a book or until I can drive a car anywhere I choose or go and see the boys.

December 14, 1999

Pamela,

I have a new job in my new housing unit. I polish the brass doorknobs on the offices in the staff hallway. It's not as much responsibility as running a mortgage company, but the pay is commensurate with the task. I make 12 ½ cents an hour. I can't complain. At least I'm not contributing to the unemployment rate in this country. I wonder if they count inmates in the unemployment figures. It probably depends whether it's a Democrat or a Republican in office.

I finally have a pal! His name is Ted. It feels weird saying that I have a pal or a friend in prison. I know you know what I mean, because you're my girlfriend and we know each other pretty well. I always think that people assume there's all this sexual assault in prison by some thug named Bubba. It's simply not true. The thug's name is Bradley. Anyhow, I'm glad to have a new friend; someone with my same sense of humor and someone with whom to make fun of the plethora of morons in here.

Ted is (was) a drug smuggler. He got caught flying weed up to Minnesota from Mexico. It would be kind of hard for him to say he didn't do it, so he doesn't deny it. He looks like your average college kid. He actually graduated from a college in Minnesota (see, we're not all college dropouts). I asked him what his major was. He joked, "I graduated with a degree in drug-smuggling." I didn't get it so he said, "I graduated with a double major; one in aviation and one in Spanish." And that's not a joke.

See you this weekend.

December 17, 1999

Pamela,

You know how some of the guys see us walking around in the outside corral of the visiting room when you're here? Well, first of all, they think you're a hot. Big surprise. Anyhow, they're always saying that you're cheating on me and that you'll never stay with me.

I'm sorry I keep talking about this, but I keep hearing how inmates get dumped by their ladies. I know you assured me, but how do you know how you'll feel in a week, a month, two months one year? I mean, you can understand my thinking, right? I'm not encouraging you to go out and find someone else. But just promise me one thing: If you feel the need to find some other companionship, please let me know beforehand. You can do anything you want out there and I'll never know. We both know that.

I know you said that you have no interest in seeing other people, but neither one of us knew what it would be like with me in here. Maybe you've changed your mind. I don't know. Maybe I'm thinking crazy. I don't know.

See you soon.

December 23, 1999

Pamela,

Thanks for putting me at ease when you came to visit me last weekend. I believe you. Not because I have to. Because I don't have to. I *want* to believe you. I love you.

December 25, 1999

Pamela,

I can't believe it's Christmas and I don't get to see a Christmas tree or give any presents. I can't describe how terrible it feels to not be with the boys or get them presents. At least Karen is accepting collect calls from me so I can speak with them once in a while. I'm sorry I can't give you anything either. It's great that you are here in Yankton this Christmas weekend.

It was cool today that they let you come onto the compound to go to the holiday service in chapel with me. The choir was pretty good, wasn't it? I've been thinking of joining it. Also, thanks for sending in the new *Star Trek* book. Hopefully, it will help me pass the time and take my mind off the holidays.

Merry Christmas, again.

December 31, 1999

Pamela,

It's the eve of Y2K. You are only about a mile away in your hotel room. As luck would have it, we can't be together. No one knows what will happen to the technology systems around the world tonight. If you get this letter it means that the power grid in Yankton, South Dakota stayed on, the inmates are not running the asylum and the prison stayed open.

January 1, 2000

Hey,

Happy New Year. Damn. I'm still here.

January 6, 2000

Pamela,

We had an "assembly" in the gymnasium today. You know, like in high school when there is a talent show? I guess they're really trying to keep us busy or entertained or something. The gospel choir did a couple of numbers. Man, they're good. Some guys read poems. I thought I'd be real smart and do a little stand-up. Bad idea! I know I was doing pretty well on the outside before I came in here, but there was a little more pressure today. I need to get better at my rhythm and flow. I've got to learn not to pause too long between jokes. I did that today, and it gave the loud mouths an opportunity to heckle me. At times, the crowd laughed harder at the hecklers than at me. Since being a loud mouth moron is so infectious, the whole place started to erupt into shouting and hollering. They yelled stuff like, "Come on, come on, *come on!* Let's go! Make us laugh, funny boy!" I thought I'd do better with a "captive" audience. (They didn't laugh at that one either.)

I think I'll just join the choir.

January 10, 2000

Pamela,

Ted and I have started to write a screenplay. It's a comedy about a 23-year-old guy named Gary, who realizes he has the powers of Jesus. He doesn't want the powers because it scares him, and he's intimidated at the idea of saving all the people on the planet. At first, he does a lot of silly miracles, just to prove to himself that he really does have these powers, but he's still scared. He's watched all the movies about Jesus and he doesn't like the way they end. A rich tycoon with political aspirations dupes him into working for him and convinces Gary to, unwittingly, do things to help the tycoon become president of the United States. Just before the tycoon wins the presidential election, Gary gets wise to the tycoons tricks and exposes the whole thing on Oprah. Since everyone in the U.S. watches Oprah, they all witnessed this brave act of stopping the voters from electing this rotten scoundrel (because the country has never elected a rotten scoundrel – ha!). The whole country saw Gary's good deed and it renewed their want to do good things themselves and to treat each other with kindness. Seeing this, God came down and relieved Gary of his savior obligations, because when Gary brought the country together on Oprah, he accomplished what he was supposed to do. I think we're going to call it, "What Would Gary Do."

What do ya think?

January 15, 2000

Sweetheart,

My prison counselor and I had that conference call with Karen and the Child and Family Services Department of Wisconsin. They convinced her that either you or my mom can bring the boys out! They convinced her that it would be okay every five weeks. It's better than nothing. I can't wait to see them.

So far I've written to about thirty people in my address book, excluding family. I've only had responses from six. That's 20 percent. I feel like I've been forgotten about. This sucks. Whatever, I guess I'm getting a better response percentage than a direct-mail marketing campaign.

January 20, 2000

Hey you!

I talked to the staff in the education department and they said that if I put together a curriculum for a twelve-week course on improvisation, they'll let me teach improv classes. They agreed it would be a good thing after I told them about how improv teaches self-esteem and communication skills. It's something a lot of people need around here. I convinced them that it will help people get jobs after they get out. They agreed. Anyhow, please send me your improv curriculum. This could be my new job! Obviously my improv training is now paying off. Thank you. I really appreciate all you are doing for me. I mean it!

January 27, 2000

Pamela,

After dinner last night, Ted and I worked on our screenplay. We went up to our room for the 10:00 count and then went back down to the classroom to continue working for another couple hours.

There was a group of other guys in there, on the opposite side of the room having what they would call; a "Bible study." One of them was the same guy who came into the TV room last week and told me to leave because he wanted to watch *Springer*. Anyway, me and Ted didn't get a whole lot done, because the nature of their meeting was nothing short of fantastic.

We had a feeling that this was going to be a once-in-a-lifetime opportunity – the eavesdropping on this bible study. We decided to memorialize the event by feverishly scribbling on to paper, the testimony.

You see, A lot of guys "find God" when they come in here. That's great; I'm not against God by any means. But, here we go.

This is what we were able to write down:

> Prisoner 1: Here's the thing - Jesus was pissed at them Jehovahs Witnesses so he and God wiped them out.
>
> Prisoner 2: When was that?
>
> Prisoner 1: Back in them Bible times. I'm not exactly sure, but it was like ten or twenty thousand years ago.
>
> Prisoner 3: There wasn't no Jehovahs back then. The Jehovahs was like seven, eight hundred years ago.
>
> Prisoner 1: That ain't what the Bible say. Bible say it was Jesus or God – or no, it was, like, Moses. I don't know, but it was some dude like that. Some cat wiped out them Jews, like two, three hundred years ago.
>
> Prisoner 3: You said it was the Jehovahs.
>
> Prisoner 2: Wasn't Jews and Jehovah's – wasn't they the same thing?

Prisoner 1: No, they ain't. That ain't what the Bible say. I read it and God wrote this whole damn book and He right.

Prisoner 3: (stands up)
Man, you a dumb ass. The Pope basically wrote it. He rewrote a lot if it because he found out things was different back then.

Prisoner 1: (stands up)
Sit down. (throws Bible at Prisoner 3) Shut up until after you read it.

Prisoner 2: (picks up Bible from floor) We could just look it up.

Prisoner 3: PUT THAT BIBLE DOWN!

The guard heard the commotion and stepped into the room. They all sat down. One of the guys turned to the guard and said that they were just studying the bible, so the guard left.

I'd never even heard of a bible study like this – with such misguided passion and ignorance. How could society have failed them so horribly? Thank God that He is an understanding deity. I think that what the bible say.

Once the guard intervened, Ted and I decided that it was a good time to leave.

It dawned on me again that I am in prison – it's easy to get complacent. If that guard hadn't come in, there may have been a fight. It's quite possible that we would have gotten dragged into it, or maybe it would have been assumed by the guard that we were somehow involved, which might have been just as bad.

I continued to be freaked out when I walked back to my cell. Since it was after the 10:00 count, the hallway on the second floor was almost pitch dark. There I was, in federal prison, walking down a dark hallway at night.

February 4, 2000

Pamela,

You know, I've hated the prosecutor on my case since the day I met him. I've always felt that I just shouldn't be here. I have been angry at the fact that he lied about some stuff, even though he had evidence that actually nailed me – legally. I've always thought he could've just let me go. As you know, I've just been mad at the federal justice system in general because I lost everything before I was officially "guilty."

But something has happened in the past couple days. I think I have found some peace. You know how I've been thinking that I "shouldn't be here"? Well, I don't want you to think I'm getting all weird on you here, but to say that I "shouldn't be here" is basically saying that the events that did take place didn't take place.

You see, right or wrong, like it or not, fair or not fair, the events that happened actually did take place! Therefore, I *should* be here. I don't know if that makes any sense at all or makes sense to anyone else, but it makes me feel better. I can't continue to think of my life starting again "once I'm out of this place." This is my life right now. For the thirty-third year of my life, I live here.

February 14, 2000

Sweetie,

Happy Valentines Day! Thank you so much for bringing the boys last weekend. It was so good to see them, but it was also so sad. They are growing up without me. Tim seemed to understand where I am, but Mikey was a little confused.

I didn't get a chance to tell you this when you were here, but since the visiting room is basically a glorified lounge, Mikey actually asked me where the "jail" was. Then when we were walking back from the kids' books area, we walked past Dave. I introduced Mikey and Tim. Later, the boys told me they had never met a real prisoner before. Thank God for youthful innocence.

I thought that the DAP class would focus on drug and alcohol abuse. It really doesn't. The focus of the class seems to be on criminal behavior and how we can go on and live our lives without living the criminal lifestyle. Seriously? What a joke. At least it's entertaining.

February 29, 2000

Yo,

Leap year! Everyone's mad around here today. As you know, the federal justice system sentences people by months. For example, a sentence can be twenty-one months or thirty-six months, etc. The big gripe around here is that today, February 29th, is an extra day in favor of the government. I guess it's a fair gripe. I'd certainly take one less day of being here.

Remember Jimmy Brock? He's one of my other cellmates – the guy who is in here for selling handguns to gang-bangers in Chicago. You met him in the visiting room last time. He was the portly guy with the seven kids who came to visit him. Anyhow, he was telling us what leap year was. He said that it is when you roll right out of one year and leap right into the next. He said, "You might leap right into February or March or something like that." He said he first "learnt" about these things when he was little and his mom's boyfriend would smack him right into next week. I don't think he was joking. I didn't know whether I should laugh or be grateful that my mom didn't date much.

March 5, 2000

Pamela,

I've been having a bad week this week. I have been really down in the dumps. Why don't my old friends from the outside write back to me? I just don't get it.

I also got in trouble. You know how my DAP class is Monday, Tuesday, Thursday and Friday, and it starts at 8:00 a.m. Every day, at 11:30 a.m. we are released. Because the chow hall is right upstairs from our classroom, our instructor usually lets us go right up to lunch – even if we haven't been called to lunch by the lieutenant over the loud speaker yet.

Today we had a substitute; it was a guard with no training in chemical dependency so class was more of a joke than it normally is. Anyway, someone told him that we usually get released early, before 11:30 so we can get up to the chow hall before the mad rush. So a bunch of us went up there a little *too* early, because one of the other DAP instructors recognized us and yanked us out of there.

This other DAP instructor played it cool and didn't report us to the lieutenant. Afterwards, he pulled five of us into his office individually and gave us each a special work assignment. We all had to write papers of varying lengths about – get this – how "going to lunch early" is part of our criminal behavior.

Seriously, we are supposed to compare and contrast "going to lunch early" with our "criminal lifestyle" and, how we are going to break this habit. Mine is supposed to be seventeen pages long. Ted only got sentenced to twelve.

When we're finished with the assignment, we're supposed to read them aloud in front of the whole

DAP class. Oh, my God, it is going to be hard not to laugh.

I can't wait to see you.

March 21, 2000

Pamela,

I can't believe you have come to visit me every weekend since I've been here. You haven't missed one! I know it is costing you so much money to stay in the hotel and gas to drive here. I mentioned a while back that people were saying you'd dump me after a month or so – because that's about the average. I want to say thanks for hanging in there and believing in me – in us. We have an interesting relationship, don't we? I mean, we've gotten to know each other and grow this relationship in a way that is quite unconventional. We just talk and write. I can't say that I prefer it this way, but our relationship isn't getting complicated by sex. So, I guess I'm saying thanks for not having sex with me.

Part of DAP class includes a fitness program. I have been walking around the track every day. When I came in here I weighed 190 pounds. I now weigh 165. Anyhow, each lap around the track is one-quarter mile. I've been keeping track of how many miles I've walked, and I am figuratively "walking back home to you". You said that it's 325 miles from prison to home. I've already walked 255 miles. I looked on a map in the library, and I am basically in Mankato, Minnesota. Only 70 more miles and I'm home!

April 8, 2000

Pamela,

Thank God there's free entertainment in here. There is this guy here we call Dobo. He's in my drug and alcohol program. He's not quite right. I feel sorry for him because I don't know if he's really all that much of a criminal. I think he's just an idiot.

His crime: He used to work for the postal service (that might explain a lot), and he somehow learned that some guys he knew were sending drugs, in packages, through the mail. Apparently he had a girlfriend who was heavily into drugs, so she talked him into stealing one of these packages. He stole the wrong package. It was drugs – in fact, it was meth – but it was a marked package that the ATF was using as a sting to catch some drug dealers. He got caught red-handed.

Anyhow, he is so fun to observe. This morning he showed up in DAP class with a buzzed head. It wasn't like a crew cut or anything; it was like someone attacked him with one of those beard trimmers – splotches and patches of short hair and some tufts of hair that weren't even touched by the buzzer. He said that he had insomnia last night so he went into the bathroom and gave himself a haircut. I can't wait until tomorrow to see what the next bout of insomnia brings.

April 23, 2000

Pamela,

When I got out of the visiting room I told Doc about your eye problem. He said it could be very serious and needed immediate attention. Since I'm only allowed to call phone numbers on my approved call list, I couldn't call you in your hotel. I had to call my mom in Minnesota, so she could call you at the hotel here in Yankton and then tell you to go to the emergency room. I don't even want to think about what would have happened if you hadn't had that emergency care. Who would have thought that a former emergency room doctor, sentenced to prison, in prison, would save the eyesight of the love of my life?

May 5, 2000

Pamela,

I don't have a whole lot to say to you. I don't know what it's going to be like when I get out of here. Who knows where my life will take me. We might not even be together. How would I know? How could anyone know for sure? I think it's possible that your definition of commitment is different than mine. You say that you know, for sure, that you want to be with me forever. How do you know? How could you possibly know? You don't know what life will deal to you or to us. Yeah, right now I'm pretty sure I want to be with you. But what if you meet someone else who is your perfect match? You think I'm the one, but how could you know, with absolute certainty that there is no one out there who is even better for you than me? This is how you feel now, but things change. I've been married before, and I was pretty damn sure she was the one. I mean, I wouldn't have gotten married if I didn't think that. Well, look what happened. It didn't work out. She wasn't the one. But I thought she was. My judgment, clearly can't be trusted. Sure, I feel like I want to be with you forever, but what if I don't feel like that in four years? What if you don't? I don't know where my head will be that far out into the future – let alone forever into the future. I can't tell you that I want to be with you forever. I do right now. But I have no idea what … Okay, now I'm just repeating myself.

And furthermore, you don't have to come here every weekend. I'm not saying that you can't come at all. I just don't want to get into fights with you in the visiting room anymore. I know it hurt you when I asked you to leave the visiting room. I didn't mean to hurt you. I felt like such a jerk. Then we couldn't talk about it until the next time you come.

I still appreciate the fact that you have come every weekend. I've never told you this before, but it's been pretty hard to adjust to being in prison when I've got one foot in the visiting room. There are a lot of things going on around here on the weekends that I don't participate in, like softball and just hanging around with the guys. If I really want to adjust, I should be part of this stuff.

We have a pretty crazy relationship. I've said before, it's great that we've gotten to know each other this way, but it isn't real. What if we can't stand each other in the real world? It's a lot different than talking in a visiting room three times a week.

If you want to skip this weekend, that would be fine.

May 11, 2000

Sweetheart,

You just left here thirty minutes ago, and I just had to write this letter now. You're an incredible person. Thank you for your dedication and understanding. You're absolutely right; we don't know that it *won't* work out. Maybe this is the best way to start a relationship. I've never done it this way before either.

Sorry I freaked you out so bad with my crazy letter last week. You had to sit with it for two days after you received it – then you had to sit in the car for five and a half hours on the way here wondering if I would show up in the visiting room when they called my name. I am so sorry.

June 5, 2000

Pamela,

I found out that if I complete DAP class, and if I don't "misbehave," I'll be able to leave here and go to the halfway house on August 21. It's good news and everything, but there it is again — that constant reminder that I'm an adult who needs to be told that I have to behave. Anyhow, this means I'll need to line up a job so I can get out on work release once I get to the halfway house. Is it possible that your improv company will be able to hire me in a marketing position and/or as an instructor? Let's talk about it when you get here this weekend.

June 23, 2000

Pamela,

I'm glad you liked the screenplay. Ted and I have another one we've started. It's not a comedy. It's about a guy who has his kidney stolen by his estranged father so he can give it to his other son. Just think of all the dynamic emotions surrounding that. We've got some work to do. We probably won't have time to type three drafts of this one, like we did with the last screenplay. Not a bad problem to have – not enough time in prison to finish typing a screenplay.

July 19, 2000

Hey Sexy,

I am sorry about last weekend. I can't believe you got kicked out of the visiting room for wearing that skirt. I know you've worn that one before, but apparently, length of skirt is the judgment call of that particular guard on duty on that particular day. Anyway, I thought you looked great. I'm also sorry that you were treated with such aggression. They have no right treating you that way. I'm the inmate. I'm the criminal. There's no reason they have to treat you like that. I am so sorry. I wish there was something I could do. I am just so powerless in here. I know you know that. Aghhhhh!

Hey, at least it wasn't me who kicked you out. I'm sorry. That's probably not funny to you.

Only a little over a month, sweetheart, and then this phase is all over. You have stuck with me throughout all of this; not missing one weekend. Other than you and my mom, I've only had a handful of visitors. I don't understand what happened to most of my friends.

Chapter 12

Halfway Home

July 20, 2000

Dear Pamela,

Only thirty-two more days and I get to leave this place! I put in my request to be incarcerated at the halfway house in Minneapolis, so at least I'll be in our hometown. On Monday, August 21st I'll be transferred to the halfway house to serve out the final six months of my sentence. Even though my sentence won't be over, at least I'll be out of here.

Here's a crazy coincidence – Ted is getting out on the same day and is probably going to the same halfway house as me, in Minneapolis.

I hope I can go to the one on Lake Street and Hiawatha. I know it's not a great neighborhood, but who cares? It's not "here." Besides, it seems a little irrational to be more concerned for my safety in a "bad neighborhood" than in prison.

I'd still like you to check with your business partner to see if I can work for you guys in some sort of marketing capacity, grant writing or something like that at the improv school. One way or another I need to find a job, or else they'll send me back here to finish my final six months. I realize both of you work out of your homes. I'm obviously not going to be allowed to do that, so if you guys decide to give me a job, you'll have to put a desk in your classroom space. You'll have to install a phone in there too, because they have to be able to get a hold of me by telephone – at any time. Mobile phones are not allowed. I guess they need to be able to check in on me to see that I'm not out there tricking more people out of money.

I still feel like such a child. I'm not saying that I shouldn't have some kind punishment for doing what I did, but now I have to come up with a new career. Quick. It's hard to see the light at the end of the tunnel. My probation doesn't even start until March 2001. From then, it's two more years before I can even set foot in a mortgage office. Even if I wanted to go back to work in the mortgage business, which I really don't think I want to, I certainly wouldn't be able to get my license back. Besides, I can't imagine someone wanting to hire a mortgage felon. I'll figure something out. Think positive, right? Things always work out.

July 24, 2000

Pamela,

Bad news. My counselor called me into her office today and told me that I won't be able to go to the halfway house in Minneapolis.

Apparently, one of the other defendants/co-conspirators from my case is currently serving his time at that halfway house. Remember during pre-trial when we heard that there were threats made by some of those other defendants?

Well, because of that, they've placed some kind of separation order in the system for all the defendants on my case. They said that the closest halfway house to Minneapolis is somewhere in Benton County, Minnesota. That's up by St. Cloud!

That's like, seventy miles away from your house; my future home. Not only that but the halfway house up there is actually the county jail, unlike the one in Minneapolis, which is an actual halfway house building with a bunch of rooms.

Every time I think I am going to get some kind of control back in my life, I am quickly reminded that based on my actions six years ago, I must be treated like a child.

By the way, thanks for coming to visit me again last weekend.

August 2, 2000

Sweetheart,

Remember when I told you I was keeping track of all the laps I was making around the track so that I could walk home to you? Well, so far I've made it 298 miles. That puts me in about the third-tier suburbs of Minneapolis. With the route you take, that puts me exactly in the suburb of Shakopee. Only twenty-seven more miles, and I'm home! It's a little anticlimactic since I'll be at that other halfway house, but it's the thought that counts. Right?

There's this guy here who I met about five months ago. He's in here for embezzling money from some big insurance company. He's always trying to "hypothetically" ask me about how to tie mortgages and real estate into some new scam he's been cooking up. I've been careful about what to tell him. I keep saying that I'll have to think about it. I can't tell him that I don't know how to do it because then he might think I'm a cop. You know what happens to someone in here when they're suspected of being a cop.

Here's the thing; I do know how to do it. I mean, of course I'm not going to get involved, but it made me realize something. Most people in the mortgage business would know how to pull something like this off – and probably not get caught. But either you're a criminal or you're not.

I've learned the hard way - it boils down to ethics, honesty and integrity. Oh, and a healthy understanding of what happens to your life when you cross the line. I swear to God Honey, we could probably write a book on this. I wish I would have understood this crap six years ago.

August 9, 2000

Pamela,

I'm so confused and nervous about this halfway house thing. Most of my drug dealer and drug smuggler friends in here have been to county jails. They say that they would prefer six months of being here in Yankton over two weeks in a county jail. And as you know, this place is not a breeze. But I have to think about the distance from Minneapolis. The county jail in Benton County is a lot closer than this place. Being there would make it easier for you and my family to come and visit. I'll still be able to get out on work release if I go there. I don't know. Let's talk about it this weekend.

August 14, 2000

Baby!

You are not going to believe this! My counselor called me into her office this morning and told me that now I *am* going to the halfway house in Minneapolis! Apparently, the defendant from my case who was staying there got busted for drugs or something and got sent to prison. Oh, how terrible for him. So sorry, idiot. Things seem to be falling into place. Can I still have that job? Tell your business partner that his wisecrack about hiring me was very funny — agreeing to pay me double what I'm making in here. Can you guys really afford 24 cents an hour?

August 15, 2000

Sweetheart,

I need to explain some technicalities to you. The halfway house falls under the jurisdiction of the Federal Bureau of Prisons. The move itself is not really a release; it's a furlough transfer. This only means that I don't have to be in cuffs and chains during the transport and I don't have to be transported by a federal marshal.

Here's the part you won't like; they'll only release me to an actual family member.

I am so sorry. I'm sure this feels insulting. You've come to see me every weekend for the past ten months. Maybe you and my brother can drive here next Monday, separately. Then I can ride with you to Minneapolis while he follows. I think my brother will do that for us. We'll be okay.

They said I'll be released for my transfer next Monday at 10:00 a.m. That's only 146 hours and thirty-two minutes from now! See you this weekend for the last time in the visiting room!

August 21, 2000

Pamela,

By the time you get this letter I'll be living only four miles from our house. Wow. It's weird saying "our" house. Its 4:30 in the morning right now, and I only have five and a half hours left in here. I haven't slept all night. I know I'll be with you soon, and we can talk about all this, but I need to get some thoughts on paper now.

I guess I'm scared. Unless someone has been in this situation before, he couldn't possibly understand how much anxiety I feel right now. All of the freedoms, as well as the responsibilities of life that I haven't had for the past ten and a half months, will now start coming back.

Of course I want to get out of here, but for the past year, this has been my life and my home. In here, I have made friends, figured out how the system works, found my place in this community, and oddly enough, I've settled in.

I also know how our relationship works from here – you come to visit on the weekends and then you go home. But now all that will change. I guess I am no different from most other people in that I have a fear of the unknown – even if the perceived unknown is better than the known.

I'm stuffed right now with so many questions and fears. What am I going to do about a long-term career? Will the business world look past my label as a felon to see who I am? Who am I? What will my relationship be with my kids? Have I lost them? What about my friends? Will they want to hang around with me again? Will I want to hang around with them – especially the ones who forgot about me while I was here? And the biggest question of all, what about us?

I thought I understood my punishment at the sentencing hearing: prison time, restitution, probation, revocation of voting rights and revocation of my right to bear arms. But I never would have dreamt the unwritten punishments would be this terrifying.

In five hours and fourteen minutes I'll walk out of here – not a free man.

Chapter **13**

House Away from Home

August 21, 2000

Hello, journal! It's been so long. I haven't written in here – talked to you – since the morning of November 4, 1999, the day I left for prison. I'm okay. Thanks for asking. I realize now that even though prison was awful, it was no where near as horrible as my pre-trial. I'm out now. I'm all the better for getting through that phase. But here we go into another.

I made it to the halfway house here in Minneapolis on time. The furlough transfer papers *commanded* that I spend no more than 7 hours getting here from Yankton. We didn't risk it. I made it in six, which didn't leave much time for fooling around – if you know what I mean. Apparently, if I hadn't made it here in the allotted time, they'd have placed me on "escape status."

That would have been embarrassing and difficult to explain. My prison buddies would say, "Hey, Mayne, we heard you escaped." Then I'd have to say, "Ahhh, no. Actually, I was just tardy."

I'm glad Pamela mailed some clothes to the prison for me before I left so I didn't have to wear that drab, crappy, khaki prison-issue uniform when I left. I couldn't believe how awkward it felt to wear my favorite jeans again. They were a little too big, but it was awesome.

Leaving that place was so strange. After putting on my own clothes, I made that walk from Receiving and Discharge to the front gate, just like I'd seen other guys do on their last day.

I know what it looks like to see an inmate on his release day walk across the prison compound, escorted by the guards, wearing real clothes instead of the drab khakis. I always wondered what they were thinking.

Today it was me making that walk and wearing clothes with color. And at exactly 10:08 a.m., Central Standard Time, I walked out of the federal prison at Yankton, South Dakota.

I asked the guards if I could have my ride wait for me a mile or so down the road. I told the guards that it had been a dream of mine to see what it would feel like to run out the front gate and never look back. They told me to shut up and get in the car.

Just before I got into the car, I looked back at the prison and saw Kirby and Gary behind the fence, working with the grounds keeping crew up there on the hill. There they were, wearing their khakis. They waved, and I waved back. I'll miss those guys. Kirby gets out in two weeks. I know what he was dreaming. Gary has four more years. He doesn't dare to dream yet.

I had two cars waiting for me. Pamela had hers and my brother had his. I gave Pamela a big hug and I so badly wanted to get into her car, but I knew the guards were watching so I got into my brother's car.

It was actually scary driving down the street at first. We were only traveling at about thirty-five miles an hour, but it seemed like a hundred. It occurred to me that my body had not traveled that fast in almost a year.

It was weird seeing what was just a few blocks beyond the prison fence. I'd lived on no more than three square blocks, right there in the middle of the town of Yankton, South Dakota for almost a year. I didn't know there was a gas station right around the corner. It's not like I would have gone there. But – who knew!

About three towns out of Yankton we stopped at a convenience store so I could switch from my brother's car into Pamela's. Yes, we broke the rules. Before we went inside the store, Pamela reached into the glove box of her car and gave me my wallet. It was completely intact. It had my driver's license, canceled credit cards, expired medical insurance card from Mayne Mortgage and 84 dollars just as it had the day I walked into the prison.

We walked in to the convenience store and I almost fell over. I couldn't believe all the colorful products. I went up to the twelve-foot-long, five-shelf-high candy rack. I just stood there staring at the reds, greens, blues, golds and silvers of the candy with the 84 dollars in my hand. I felt like a little kid. I also had this twitch of urgency, like I had to hurry up and get my supplies and get the hell out of there before anyone discovered that there was a felon in the store. So, I grabbed a whole case of candy cigarettes, paid for them at the counter and left. I haven't had candy cigarettes in about twenty years. It wasn't even my candy of choice back then.

And just like that, I put 23 dollars and 67 cents back into the economy.

When we crossed the border from South Dakota into Minnesota, I rolled down the window and shouted an expletive back at the prison. I guess I felt safe since we were about 100 miles from there.

It was such an incredible feeling, driving across Minnesota with the window down, green trees flying by and the wind gushing in the window. We didn't talk about anything important, just this and that. It reminded me of the road trip we took to L.A. just a month before I had to go to prison. I didn't want it to end.

We finally arrived at the halfway house. I said goodbye once again to Pamela. It was an optimistic good-bye, but still sad. She's only a few miles from here. I just keep telling myself, "Only six more months."

I am finding it hard to calm down and go to sleep tonight in my new digs. I am so amazed at how amazed I've been all day. It's probably just sensory overload. You'd think I've been down for ten years or something, but it's only been just under a year.

They said that tomorrow I can get privileges to take a walk outside, unsupervised! They said that I have to stay on the south side of Lake Street and can walk down only as far as the Mississippi River. I can't believe how insane that sounds – a half a mile there and back. Unsupervised. No guards. I'll believe that when it happens.

I know this sounds crazy, but I keep thinking that someone will see me out there walking down the sidewalk and call the FBI to report a criminal on the loose. I can't wait until I snap out of this.

Ted made it here too. At least I have my prison pal. We can keep working on that second screenplay.

Chapter 14

The End of the Tunnel

August 24, 2000

It's been a few days now and I'm settling in here at the halfway house. Ted and I got the best room – right by the front door. Everyone thinks we're gay. Yeah, I was one of the few inmates to have a girl visit me every weekend. So I'm gay? That's so awesome.

Since we're at the front of the halfway house, we don't have to deal with the morons in the back. Even though everyone else in here are criminals transitioning from prison back into the real world, a lot of them come from higher-level prisons. Some are violent offenders and the others; I guess I just don't know. But I've gone through most of my downtime with Ted, so it's good to still have him around.

Some of the rules in here are just as humiliating as the ones at the prison. A couple times each week we have to pee in a cup for drug testing. I don't completely understand this. Sure, most of the people I have experienced in the prison system are drug dealers, drug smugglers or simply addicts. But I'm a white-collar criminal, damn it. I'm so special.

Well, I did get time off for going through that Drug and Alcohol Program in prison. Okay then, peeing in a cup in order to get time cut off my sentence – sounds good.

I have a case manager here. I don't know how one qualifies for a case manager position here but apparently, intelligence and communication skills are not required. But she's in charge of me so I have to do what she says. She said that if I behave, I'll get a forty-eight-hour hour pass to go home next weekend. Behave. The child treatment continues.

I'm a little nervous about going home. I mean, it's not really my home, it's Pamela's home. She says it's our home – I know. Maybe I just feel uncomfortable because I can't really contribute, financially, to the household. Pamela and I still have stuff to figure out about our relationship. So far, she's been through all this with me — all the driving, visiting every weekend and believing in me. Perspective.

The rules for the forty-eight-hour hour pass are very strict. Why wouldn't they be? When I think about it, I can't really believe they let us go to our homes at all. I mean, we are still serving out our federal prison sentence and are still under the jurisdiction of the Federal Bureau of Prisons.

There is a sophisticated voice-recognition computer system that can call me at home, at any time, and ask me to repeat the names of the states in the U. S. If my voice doesn't match my prerecorded template they'll send the authorities. I suppose it's better than wearing an ankle bracelet.

In a couple weeks I get to start my job with Pamela's improv school. They're hiring me as the director of marketing. They've installed a phone in their classroom space so that the halfway house can check up on me at any time during business hours. I'll be making $18,000 a year. And I'll be working *for* someone. That'll be weird. I haven't worked *for* someone since about 1994. At some point, I could ask my counselor if I can office at home. What the hell – I can ask.

Two years ago I couldn't have imagined living on $18,000 a year. Now it seems like a ton of money. It's amazing how little one needs when one has nothing.

August 28, 2000

I got a two-hour pass today to go to the store for toiletries, clothes and stuff like that. I also went to the bank to open a checking account. When I walked into the bank I realized I was shaking. I had this feeling that they'd discover, on their computer system or something, that I'd just been released from federal prison. I kept thinking that the words "fraud and money laundering" were going to flash up on their screen, and the cops would rush in and tackle me to the ground. They must have thought I was going to rob the place by the way I kept looking at the guards.

I know it's completely irrational but I can't seem to shake this feeling of guilt. It probably didn't help that I chose to bank with the institution that was the victim of my crime.

My counselor told me that I could have my first forty-eight-hour pass this weekend. That will be so weird. Pamela still has my/our bed. It's been almost a year since I've slept in that bed. Oh – my – God!

She's going to pick up the boys from Karen before she comes here and gets me for the weekend. Karen allowed them to visit four times while I was in prison, and I spoke to them every couple of weeks on the phone, but this will be different. For the first time in almost a year, they get to wake up to Dad.

September 3, 2000

Aside from the phone calls from the criminal monitoring, computer voice-recognition system at all hours of the night, my first weekend at home was incredible. Incredible doesn't even describe it. Unbelievable! I was with Pamela and the boys in a home, my home, in a real bed with real cereal and milk – my family. This must be what it feels like when God is smiling.

September 4, 2000

I started my job today! I was released from the halfway house at 7:30 a.m. I had to be back by 5:00 p.m. — which, let me just say, was long enough for the first day. I kept checking to see that there was a dial tone at work because I was afraid that the phone might go out and the halfway house wouldn't be able to get in touch with me. Then, of course, they'd have to send in the cops.

A staff member from the halfway house did in fact show up to make sure I was there. He was a kid in his early twenties. He wants to be a prison guard someday. I feel so sorry for him; so young and naïve. He said that he'll be stopping by, randomly, to check in on me.

Where in the hell do they think I'd go? And what do they think I'd do – run out to a mortgage company and write a bad loan? You know what? They probably do think that.

September 29, 2000

It's been over a month now, and I'm getting used to this halfway house routine. All in all, I have to say that I'm pretty happy to be out of the prison. My brother gave me an old rusted-out Montero so I can go back and forth from work. It's a far cry from my Mercedes, but I am not complaining. I'm so lucky that people like my brother are helping me out. I'm actually making some money and can contribute to the household.

My health benefits from my job will kick in on November 1. I'm making money, I get to go home on weekend passes, and my relationship with Pamela and my kids is starting to really take shape again.

I've settled into my room here at the halfway house with Ted. They let us have our laptops in here, and we're on the third rewrite of our second screenplay. I'm starting to feel like a real member of society again.

October 15, 2000

I can't believe it! This is so awesome. I put in a request to office out of my home, and it was granted! It never hurts to ask. Anyhow, this means that each day from 7:30 until 5:00 I'll be at home. Then, assuming I continue to behave, I can go home on my weekend passes too.

I can honestly see the light at the end of the tunnel now.

I am eligible for home confinement at the end of January 2001. This means that I can actually live at home, and I'll only have to check in with my case manager at the halfway house once a week. I'll still need to be available for the middle of the night phone calls from the criminal monitoring computer system, and I can't be out past 9:00 p.m., but I'll almost be a free man again. I'll be completely done with my sentence on March 16, 2001. Then, I start my two years of probation, which will be no big deal – at all!

I don't really think there's a future for me here at the improv school. It's a pretty small company, and I know they can barely afford to pay what they're paying me now. I do have improv and stand-up comedy experience. Maybe I'll just continue to do improv and stand-up and get on *Saturday Night Live*.

Even though there's some career uncertainty, it's good to dream again.

Chapter 15

You've Got to be Kidding

November 2, 2000

What next!

For the past week I've had a sharp pain in my right testicle. It concerned me so I called Doc, my old friend from Yankton. He got out about 6 months before I did, but I tracked him down; got a hold of him at his new job. He works at a Tires Plus in Uptown.

I described my symptoms. He calmly told me to get in to see a urologist right away. So I got permission from the halfway house and then made an appointment.

They did an ultrasound and found a big black mass in the center. He said it's a tumor and has to come out. He said he can't be certain it's cancer until they do a biopsy, and they won't do that until after the surgery.

He said that it has to come out right away because if it is testicular cancer, it can spread into the lymphatic system and then the lungs and brain really fast. He's been a urologist for over fifteen years and said that he's pretty sure it's cancer. My surgery is scheduled for Saturday, November 4. I'm lucky my health insurance from my job with Pamela's improv company kicked in yesterday.

I'm getting tired of being the most interesting person my friends know.

November 3, 2000

It's Friday night and I'm home on a weekend pass. I told the halfway house about my surgery and they said that it's okay if I have it over the weekend. They said I don't have to be back until the doctor releases me from the hospital, which will probably be some time on Sunday. The halfway house said that they'll expect to see me back there by Sunday night.

I talked to my counselor about letting me stay at home to recover until Wednesday or Thursday. They did not grant my request. They said that the alternative is to transfer to the federal prison in Rochester, Minnesota, which is actually a prison medical facility. I'd rather not go there. That's where the crazy criminals go to stay and the old criminals go to die. I guess I really wouldn't care who is there, but it's still prison and I'd be locked up again. I'm already halfway out, so no thanks.

I'll stay at the halfway house on the weeknights and I'll home office on the weekdays. The doctor said that I wouldn't be able to drive for a while so Pamela said she'd come and pick me up and take me home every day.

This is just unbelievably bad luck. Tomorrow morning I'm going in for surgery to remove what is almost certainly a cancerous tumor. What the hell? Cancer? Now I have cancer? How in the hell did I get cancer? Man, I'm having a bad couple-a years.

If it is cancer, I wonder how long I've had it. I did some cancer research on the internet tonight and it appears to be pretty serious. I read that compared to other types of cancer, they have a real good handle on testicular cancer, and they know how it works. They know how it spreads and they know how to stop it. That's good. But I guess people die from this. Lance Armstrong had testicular cancer and he's still alive. I wonder if I'll need chemotherapy.

November 5, 2000

I was released from the hospital at noon today and rested at home until 4:30 p.m. Then Pamela brought me back here to the halfway house. She was with me the whole time at the hospital. She slept in the chair Saturday night. She took care of me today at home. What have I done to deserve her?

The guys here at the halfway house have been stopping by my room tonight to see how I'm doing. Ted has taken over as the host for our room. He bought me the book written by Lance Armstrong about testicular cancer. I have a good friend here.

The doctor said I'll feel better by the end of the week. I'll be able to get up and about pretty easily. He's got me on some pretty heavy narcotic pain killers. That's good. Keep 'em comin'.

November 9, 2000

I went back in to see the doctor today. Their tests proved the tumor was in fact cancerous. My doctor said that it's an extremely aggressive form of cancer that has probably spread into my lymphatic system. He said that he highly recommends another surgery. The next step is to go in and remove select lymph nodes from the chest and abdominal cavity.

He wasn't trying to scare me, but he said that it's a procedure that ranks right up there with open-heart surgery. Of *course*, it does.

Isn't life divine.

We've scheduled the second surgery for the day after Thanksgiving. The doctor said that I'll probably be recovering in the hospital for a week to a week and a half. The halfway house said that as soon as they let me out of the hospital, I'll need to get back to the routine. After all, this *is* still my sentence.

I can see some similarities between this cancer and the whole prison thing. Once the events of the crime were in motion, there was no way to reverse or change course. In the same way, now that this cancer illness has started, there is no way to reverse or change course.

The one big difference is that I set the criminal events in motion. And with the cancer, I had nothing to do with its onset. However, once in motion, the feeling of powerlessness is overwhelming.

November 20, 2000

I am scared because I have cancer. I know people die from cancer. But now I've had time to think about this. For some reason, I just know that everything will be all right. I just don't see myself dying right now.

November 27, 2000

I'll spend my 34th birthday in the hospital. So, I'll say happy birthday to myself now. I'm really trying not to be scared. Pamela is here. I heard somewhere that true wisdom, is knowing when to rely of the strength of others.

December 7, 2000

The second surgery went well. They removed several cancerous lymph nodes. I guess one was the size of a golf ball and it was lodged up near my heart. The incision runs from below my waist up to my sternum and it hurts. Thank God and science for painkillers.

I really don't remember much from the first couple days after the surgery. The morphine drip kept me pretty much out of it. I had brief visions of Jeff, when he was dying seven years ago at home.

I have sketchy memories of a few days ago when my heartbeat spiked and a bunch of nurses and doctors rushed into my room. I thought of John dying of a heart attack two years ago. I wonder if Mom thought she was going to loose a third son this time around.

I remember the nurse forcing me to get up and walk just a couple of days after my surgery. I hated her then, but now I know how important it was.

I remember, every time I opened my eyes, Pamela was right there.

December 8, 2000

Pamela dropped me off at the halfway house tonight. I didn't know if I was going to make it up the steps. This is so ridiculous. Can't I just go home? Haven't I had enough punishment for my crime? I really just want to go home.

December 9, 2000

Pamela suspected she was pregnant and as it turns out, she is. She went to the doctor and apparently she conceived at the end of October. That was just before my diagnosis. People are calling it a miracle baby. I am too.

A baby. Wow. We are going to have a baby. It'll be my third, her second. So, we'll have four kids between the two of us.

I can see it now. My stand-up comedy bio:

Jerome hails from a small, Midwest, Catholic farming community. He lives each day under a veil of guilt, wondering if his mother will ever forgive him for dropping the bowl of mashed potatoes during the big Christmas dinner. Since leaving his hometown he has had kids, been married, had kids, got divorced, went to prison, got out, had kids, and now finds that comedy is his best form of therapy. His life is the chronology for the true trailer park handbook.

None of my boys will ever wear a mullet. If they do, they'll be kicked out of the trailer home immediately!

December 14, 2000

Pamela has been coming to the halfway house every morning by 7:30 to pick me up and bring me home to the home office. I can't drive my vehicle because it's a stick shift and surprisingly, you have to use your stomach muscles to push in the clutch and shift gears.

December 16, 2000

Today I started a six-week program of chemotherapy. I feel a little crappy tonight, and I'm told it will get much worse. The doctor prescribed me something called Marinol. I guess the pills are like marijuana. Yeah, the staff here at the halfway house loves me now — I am the only guy in here who has permission from the doctor to test positive for drugs.

December 18, 2000

I was called in to my case manager's office to discuss the results of my most recent drug test. She said I tested positive for heroin and pot, and that this is how inmates get sent back to prison. I asked her to check my file and look at the prescriptions from my oncologist, for the Hydrocodone and Marinol. Does she have a brain? How many fingers am I holding up?

December 25, 2000

Last Christmas I was in prison. The Christmas before that, I sat around telling my family about a bogus indictment that I'd be able to explain my way out of. This Christmas I just sat on the couch, like the Grinch in the middle of Whoville, while my family opened presents and ate roast beast.

I'm disappointed. Not because I can't keep my mind on what Christmas is really about – Jesus' birthday. It's just that all this crap is getting to me.

I'm disappointed because my body stopped working properly. For some reason, select few cells in my body got all freaked out and started reproducing way too fast. This cell behavior became more and more popular among the cell communities within my body. My lymphatic system did its best at containing these confused cells. It did this by putting them into their nodes. My urologist and oncologist thought that the lymphatic system had put up a good fight. Bravo; good job, men. But, the doctors couldn't be sure. So, they decided to send in the smart chemicals – the chemo chemicals – the chemicals that poison my body. These smart chemicals hunt for those radically reproducing cells and kill them. Oh, but there's just a few other things I've noticed, other than not having a right testicle. Since hair follicles have cells that rapidly reproduce, they get killed too. White-blood cells also fit this rapid-cell-reproducing profile. They get mis-fingered and many of them are tragically and unjustly killed. The other systems in my body recognize these chemicals as poisonous. And as such, most of the energy in my body is used to fight off this poison. It is, however, a controlled poison, and it's saving my life.

January 7, 2001

I've got to remember to keep writing in here. With the chemo every week, my fix of pain killers and my pot pills keeps me in a fog. With all the drugs

I'm on, I can't really remember what happens from one day to the next.

The thought of going off pain killers is scary. Even the days I'm not in a lot of pain, I find myself counting the hours until I can take the next pill. When I run low on pills, I find myself counting out the pills.

I count out the four-hour intervals of my waking hours. Like right now, I have seven more whole pills of Vicoden. I usually break them in half and take a half a pill every two hours, instead of one every four.

It's 8:30 now. I just took half of a pill and in a bit here, I'll go to bed. I'll take a whole one when I wake up tomorrow morning – probably around 7:00. Then I'll take a half-one at around 10:00, then a half every two hours for the rest of the day. That's four whole pills per day. By 6:00 p.m., the day after tomorrow, I'll be out of pills. I can get another refill tomorrow when I go in for my chemo. I've tried to hide some pills from myself, but that doesn't really work because I find myself counting those into the total when I calculate. I don't know what I'll do when they won't give me anymore prescriptions. I suppose, after my next refill of Vicoden, I can tell my doctor that those pills are starting to make me feel nauseous and then he'll prescribe a different pill, like Hydrocodone. This way I can start to stockpile.

I'll eventually run out. I don't want to think about it. I know this sounds insane; the fear of running out of pills. I try to justify the need for the pills by telling myself that I *need* then; I just had major surgery a month ago. I mean seriously, my incision is about a foot and a half long. Of course it's going to hurt when someone cuts through all my abdominal muscles. I deserve these pills, right?

What am I hiding from?

January 14, 2001

A couple weeks ago I was telling Ted how weird it would be here at the halfway house by myself when he goes on home confinement. He's supposed to leave for home confinement in a couple days. They'll probably put someone else in the room with me. God only knows what kind of loser it will be.

So here's the thing, maybe its because Ted's not looking forward to going to live with his dad – I don't know, but he said he'd stay here an extra 10 days until I go on home confinement on the 24th. I couldn't find the words to describe my appreciation.

I remember my step-father telling me, reluctantly, of being in Korea and how the guys there got through their hell with their war buddies. On their downtime they found ways to laugh together – no doubt in order to stay sane through the terror. They watched out for each other in battle and from time to time, they saved each other's lives.

I know that what I've gone through isn't military battle. I know there could never be a medal for bravery, nor would there be an honorable discharge for serving out my time. But on the inside, Ted and I got through this together, and I'll never forget that.

January 21, 2001

I get to move out of the halfway house to go on home confinement. I get to serve the final month and a half at home. Pamela is planning a whole day at home – just the two of us – candles lit, shades drawn, music low.

February 1, 2001

It has not been hard to get used to being in my own bed every night this past week.

I only have to deal with my counselor twice a week. God, she's an idiot. She found two old car radios in the back seat of the car that my brother is letting me use. These radios look like they were ripped out of a '71 Impala from some junkyard. I don't know why they were in there. My brother builds cars – I suppose that's why. He probably just had them lying around.

At first I thought she was going to accuse me of stealing them. Nope. She reminded me that we're not supposed to have cell phones. Then she said that having these two radios were against the rules because I *could* hook them together and make a cell phone. So she confiscated them! I've gotta believe that she watches too many MacGyver reruns. Now that I think about it, I'm glad she didn't notice that I have a watch and a belt. I'm planning to make a spaceship so I can escape this filthy, rotten planet.

February 5, 2001

I think I've finally snapped out of the pain-killer addiction; the withdrawal. It was a week from hell, and I almost lost Pamela. I told her I was going to move out. I don't know how she can put up with me. Either she's a glutton for punishment, or she knows something about us that I don't.

February 10, 2001

Only one more month until the end of my sentence! I still have the phone calls from the criminal computer monitoring system at all hours of the night. I still can't be out past 9:00, but at least I get to sleep in my own bed. I realized that, ironically, I was allowed to go on home confinement the same week my chemotherapy ended. Real funny. Perfect timing.

I've been able to go to some of the open-stages to work on my stand-up comedy again. I especially like Pepito's since it's only two and a half blocks from the house. I can get there by 6:00, work on my set, go on and do my five minutes, watch some of the other comics and then be home by my 9:00 curfew.

I have to keep reminding myself that even though I'm on home confinement, I'm still serving my federal prison sentence. It's a risk being at the open stage, which is also a bar.

The criminal computer monitoring system keeps me honest to see if I'm obeying my curfew. I can't drink at the bar, or anywhere else for that matter. Sometimes I'd like to. I don't know. I mean, I did go through nine months of that drug and alcohol program while I was locked up. I don't think I've ever really had an alcohol problem. Maybe I do.

Anyhow, I really want to get my comedy chops back. Pamela is such a great cheerleader and comedy coach. It helps that for all of her adult life, and even a few years before that, she's been involved in the improv and stand-up comedy business. Safe to say she knows what's funny and what's not.

It's weird seeing some of the guys who were just starting stand-up when I was, two years ago. I can tell they're farther along than I am. They've developed their stage presence and they're funnier. I feel like I'm playing catch-up. Sometimes I find myself thinking that for the past year and a half, the world stopped. That life was on hold. But situations like this slap me back into reality and remind me that life didn't stop. Things developed and changed all around me.

Some of my pre-prison stand-up pals ask me where I've been. They say that they thought I simply quit comedy, gave up like so many other people do. It's kind of funny, they were there when I was getting ready to go to prison. I talked about it for months before I left. They were there. Did they think I was just making it up? Or was I so self-centered that I thought that the things going on in my life should have been more important to them?

I feel stupid and a little ashamed of the fact that I was away in prison. I mean, it was actually prison. Everyone knows that only "bad" people go to prison, right? I find myself minimizing the hell that it was. I find myself telling them that I actually had fun. I joke about it like it was good to get away for a while. I tell them that I got a lot of good comedy material there in prison. Well, that part is true. I still tell people that I got screwed by the system; set up, as if I really didn't do anything wrong. I wonder how long I will continue to do that?

How long will it be until I truly accept the fact that my choices, over six years ago, hurt people and have irreversibly changed my life? I think back. I did some things that were unethical. And for the most part, I've even accepted the fact that I was committing a crime. But who would have thought this would happen? Will I ever regain my dignity, my self-worth, and my self-confidence? Why don't they teach this in the Business 101 courses? Perhaps this lesson is only taught in the upper-level Life courses.

February 28, 2001

My God. A year ago I was locked up. I was being told when to get up, when to go to breakfast, when I could have the lights on, when to go to the bathroom, when to stand there and be quiet so I could be counted. I had to be concerned, on an hourly basis, about not looking at someone the wrong way.

I still have those times when I look around at this freedom and find myself so amazed at the fact that I was actually in prison.

Pamela's pregnancy is progressing just swimmingly and the miracle baby will be born in July. I still can't believe we're actually having a kid. I have to admit, the odds were slim. Life keeps twisting and turning. I can't wait to see the little guy.

I assume history will repeat itself. I've had two *best days of my life*. Once when my first boy was born, and then again when my second boy was born. I just can't wait to see his little face. What will he be like? It's nice to have something great like this to look forward to — yes, another *best day of my life*.

The doctor said my hair will start growing back in a few weeks, and I'll start to regain the weight I've lost. I'll be checking in with him pretty regularly over the next year or two to make sure that the cancer is gone.

What am I going to do with my life? I've been through a lot, made a lot of stupid choices, and I feel I'm getting good at handling the crazy things that come my way. I've got an incredible partner in Pamela and a new baby on the way. I keep thinking, "What next?"

March 16, 2001

My sentence is over! I am done with the Federal Bureau of Prisons. No more calls from the halfway house criminal computer monitoring system at all hours of the night. It was a little anticlimactic since I was eased out of it by going from prison to the halfway house, then to home confinement. I'm not complaining though.

Pamela is organizing a celebration at Bull's tonight. It'll be weird because I haven't been out past 9:00 p.m. in sixteen and a half months. About a dozen of my old friends will be there. After that, Pamela and I are getting a hotel room downtown. I get to drink beer again. I haven't done that in sixteen and a half months either. That'll be so weird.

Chapter 16

Just on Paper

March 28, 2001

My probation officer is so cool. Coincidentally, Ted and I have the same one. I only have to visit her once a month. I have to maintain a job, and continue to pay on my $144,000 in restitution to the victim, Wells Fargo. I'll have to turn in a financial report at the end of each month so that they can see if I am making too much money. I can't take illegal drugs. I can't leave the state without written permission from the United States Probation Office. If I don't follow these rules I will not pass go, nor collect the $200. I will go directly back to prison. And of course I still can't own a gun.

I also have to start paying my child support again. It's supposed to be 25 percent of my monthly income or $500, whichever is greater. With my salary of $1,500 a month, the child support represents over a third of my gross income. Pursuant to the divorce decree, I am also required to maintain health and life insurance policies on both of my boys, and continue to pay restitution. Thank God, Pamela has a job so I don't have to pay rent and utilities.

I don't think this job with Pamela's improv company will last too much longer. With this position, I'm really on my own. I mean, I talk to her and her business partner about — generally — what I'm supposed to be doing, but it's not like Pamela acts as my boss. I mean, she's my girlfriend. Besides, marketing is such a broad title. I just don't seem to be the same self-starter as I used to be. I don't like to make excuses, but I think that the whole indictment, losing my business, losing my self-esteem, prison, cancer – all that crap still has me down.

I'll get it back. I know I will.

July 10, 2001

The third best day of my life! The miracle baby, Jeffrey Michael, was born today. We took the name of brother Jeff, who passed away in 1993, and the name Mike from Pamela's brother.

August 5, 2001

It's full speed ahead as a comic. Yeah, it's a long shot, I know. At least this is one career where my felony record won't keep me from getting work. Hell, substance abuse, criminal record; I fit right in. Pamela knows this life. She's been around comics her whole life. She has seen dozens of people come up through the ranks, go on the road and burn out in a year or two.

It's not like I don't believe her. It makes sense. Ninety-nine percent of all stand-up gigs are in bars, where it's quite convenient to drink.

I don't like to believe I'm just like everyone else. I don't think I'll fail or burn out. I wonder why she doesn't see that in me? She says that even if I am one in a thousand who actually makes it, success in this business means being away from home. I suppose she's got a point.

So, what else am I supposed to do for work? What other career am I qualified for? I've looked into some and have gone on interviews. I think I'm most qualified to be in the mortgage business, but since I'm still on probation I'm not even allowed to be a receptionist in a mortgage office. What to do? What to do?

October 28, 2001

I got booked as the feature act at a comedy room up in Dickinson, North Dakota last week. It was 500 miles each way, and I got $125 and a hotel room for doing thirty minutes of material. I was on the road driving for a total of twenty hours. I was actually at the hotel up there for eleven hours. Pamela told me that this is how it works. I understand. I didn't expect to get my own sit-com in the first year. She is being very supportive and letting me discover the ups and downs of stand-up.

I need to make money, and that's all there is to it. I wish I hadn't convinced myself that I wasn't qualified to be in any other line of work. I've just got to get past this. Pamela has been suggesting that I consider the idea of public speaking and telling my story. I suppose it would have helped if I'd heard a story like this 10 years ago.

We talked about me doing this a while ago, and I put together a rough outline. I might as well give it a shot. What else am I going to do? I suppose I just need to start calling mortgage companies and mortgage associations to see if they think my story could actually help their people. I don't know how much someone would pay me to do something like this. If they want me at all, I'm sure it would pay more than stand-up. In the meantime, I at least have some stand-up gigs coming up — $50 here, $100 there.

December 11, 2001

Pamela is really getting tired of me going to so many open stages each week. I understand the frustration, but this is my occupation. I know it is tough sitting home with the kids three or four nights a week while I am out at these comedy clubs, but what else does she want?

I got a list of mortgage associations off the internet. I should just start calling them. I am too scared and ashamed to ask the Minnesota mortgage associations. I'm sure they hate me. All they know is that I was involved in that fraud conspiracy case a couple years ago and that I pled guilty and went to prison. I just assume that they all think I'm just a bad guy. I just have this huge reluctance to make the sales calls to get work. I guess I don't want the rejection. And I definitely don't want to be judged again.

I need to quit whining about it, I know that. I need to get to a place where I can embrace this whole thing. It would probably be therapeutic for me to put it out there and admit to my former peers that, yes, it was me. I committed the crime.

I did it, and if you decide to cross the line like I did, here's what will happen. Here are the real consequences of fraud. Here is the unwritten sentence. I am not a hero for standing up here talking to you. I committed a crime. I contributed to the negative impression the public sometimes has on your industry. There is a victim, a business out there who lost $144,000 because of my involvement in a conspiracy to commit fraud. That is not commendable.

Maybe this could work. I'm sure I'll have critics who will look at it as if I'm just trying to make money off my crime. They would not be completely wrong. But I am qualified for this line of work.

March 1, 2002

I'm in! I got my first speaking gig for a mortgage association in Indiana. It isn't until May. I am so nervous. What if they blast me for being a bad guy in their industry? I'll just have to be prepared for it. I'll just have to take it. But they hired me, and they know what I did. They've seen my résumé. I think I made it quite clear that I am a criminal and that I am going to talk about the consequences of committing fraud. My brother came up with a good name for my talk: "Know Fraud, No Felony". I can't back out now; I've signed a contract.

May 12, 2002

I did it! I told my story to about 150 mortgage industry professionals yesterday. I got some pretty good feedback too. One person told me he thinks every loan officer in this business should hear my story. Maybe I have found a new profession. It is crazy to think that the only reason I am qualified is because I have been to prison. What a résumé item.

For the past few years I have allowed my self to live in shame. I'd also lost my self-confidence and dignity. While the actions of my past are truly part of my history, I vow that this will not define me. I will move forward and simply view these events as a marker for those places and times in my life.

I've never been a very religious man, but there must be some truth to the saying, "God will never give you more than you can handle." These experiences have given me an invaluable opportunity to refocus my perspective and outlook on life. I can say, for better or for worse, I will never be the same again.

In the words of one of my brilliant, former fellow inmates, "I can sum up my prison experience in *two* words – IT WAS EDUCATIONAL."

Epilogue

My desire to publish this story was in the hopes that it will raise the awareness of fraud and the consequences that lie beyond fraudulent acts. I hope you found it enlightening.

I hope that while you read, you took the time to reflect on situations in your life where you have been forced to make critical decisions. Was there impropriety? Were you parallel to my story or perpendicular? There are situations of impropriety that pop up every day in Corporate America, and I believe that it is imperative that we know the true consequences.

The primary message; there is more to a criminal sentence than the words from the judge at the sentencing hearing.

When I pled guilty, I thought my sentence was going to be several things: twenty-one months in prison, two years of probation, $144,000 in restitution, revocation of my Constitutional right to vote and the revocation of my Constitutional right to bear arms, for the rest of my life. That's all that was on the piece of paper. But as you now know, the piece of paper is just the tip of the iceberg.

I truly never saw myself as a criminal. I didn't set out to commit a crime. I actually saw myself as "Joe American." I saw myself just as many of you do: entrepreneurs, salesmen and business professionals with friends and families. I made a series of horrible choices that put me in the middle of a fraud scheme, and I chose not to call foul. I chose to be a part of it.

I was not innocent. I did it. I pled guilty and agreed to my sentence. As of the printing of this edition, it's been about twenty-two years since the commission of my crime and fifteen years since the official end of my prison sentence, and I still experience some consequences.

My prison sentence has ended, but my financial responsibility of paying restitution to the victim has not. The unwritten sentence remains and at times it still smacks me down.

Here are a few examples of how the nightmare keeps popping up.

The stigma has followed me. The feeling that I am a bad person has been hard to rise above. It was most prevalent for me in the first few months and years after I was released.

Whenever I would walk into a bank, I felt that the tellers, managers, the guards and even the customers were watching me. And that at any moment they would deny me service and possibly even call me out and arrest me. When I was out in public I would turn away from the police. By most people's definition this is completely irrational. But not to me, and it's not for those who have traveled my journey.

For a long time after I was released, I couldn't resist the urge to confess to people I met that I had been in prison. I realized one day that I was probably doing this just in case they found out later and then judged me as a societal imposter. Some people flat out told me that I was this imposter, which didn't help my self-confidence at all.

The restitution shows up as a federal judgment i.e., a lien in the county records. It also shows up as a judgment on my credit report. This is something I didn't think of when I was involved in the crime. Even after I pled guilty I didn't realize that this was going to be part of my sentence.

A few years after I was released, there was a situation in my neighborhood. I had to move out because there was drug activity going on near the house I was renting. One lovely fall morning, a few stray bullets made their way into my front door. Perhaps some dissatisfied customers were lodging their complaints about low quality products they'd purchased. I'm not sure. I am sure however that my baby boy had just tottled away from our front door, avoiding the "customer complaint" by just a few feet.

I absolutely had to move my family. But I could not qualify to rent another home because every time I filled out an application, I was asked to explain this large federal judgment. I always told the truth, and I was always turned down. Just before I decided to lie about the judgment, I ran across some incredible people who felt that I didn't need to be judged anymore.

My probation has been over for quite a while and I don't have to get permission from my probation officer to leave the state anymore. But I still remember when I had to apply for and carry a piece of paper, issued by the United States Probation Office, any time I left the state. Which meant that I had to get permission every two weeks to pick up Timmy and Mikey for my weekend visitations. They lived less than a mile across the Minnesota border, in Wisconsin. It literally took me less than fifteen minutes to pop in and out of this neighboring state to pick them up.

I was a child in the eyes of my government. I needed supervision because I couldn't be trusted to follow the laws of the land.

To those who think that cutting corners is not a big deal, because *everybody* does it; proceed at your own risk.

A man comes across, what appears to be a shortcut through the woods. The entry is clearly posted with a weathered sign that reads, *No Trespassing*. All who see this sign understands its command, yet a beaten path runs past the sign and into the woods. As far as the man can see, there are no skulls, corpses or other indications of tragedy that had befallen the carefree souls who'd crossed before. He doesn't even hear scary music as he stands at this aperture in the woods. Sure, he heard tell of a trespasser who'd found himself staring into the hollow end of old man Bjorklund's shotgun. But that was out East, or West or something.

So what does the man do?

Many of my former fellow inmates remarked that prison life was similar to the military. Physically and mentally, you can get beaten down. Sometimes your life is in danger. The rules are strict. The food is bad. The work is tedious. You get the opportunity to enjoy the camaraderie of hundreds of crass, smelly, hairy men. The folks in charge can seem less than management quality. Even the khaki uniforms we wore in prison were military surplus. But there is one big difference; there is no honor in prison. Ever.

Are these direct and incidental consequences fair? I didn't think so at the time. I still don't like what happened. But it doesn't matter what I think. It doesn't matter what you think about them either. This is how it works. If you choose to cross the line there are consequences.

Here's the good news – being a professional business-person is a great thing! Your life doesn't have to get ruined for being a part of corporate

America. You don't have to be stupid and you don't have to cut corners. There is some great training out there, so take it. There is plenty of money to be made out there. Good, honest money; so make it.

You have the opportunity, every day, to omit facts or turn the other way. Some of you, at one time or another have done or will do it. You may truly believe that it's no big deal. Maybe you were trained that way and don't know any better. Maybe you think that everybody does it and that nothing is really going to happen. Not to you; you've been in your profession for fifteen years and have put in a lot of hard work for your company. Or you're the manager or the owner and have proven that you are responsible. Maybe you have two kids and are an outstanding citizen and even volunteer at church. Beautiful. That's great. But the opportunity is still there and you're still vulnerable and eligible.

For what it's worth, coming from a felon, always be ethical, honest, diligent and consistent. Your family, friends and society, needs you to stay out of prison.

"How do you plead to the fraud charges brought against you by the United States of America?" is a question I know I'll never have to answer again.

How about you?

Jerome Mayne is an international keynote speaker and author. He works with professional associations and companies helping their people make the right decisions when the right decisions aren't easy - and stay out of prison.

In addition to speaking and writing, he is a musician, comic, and an improv comedy instructor. He lives in Eden Prairie, Minnesota with his wife Pamela. Yes, he married the girl.

Please leave an honest, thoughtful review on Amazon.com.

Contact him at: jerome@jeromemayne.com or visit www.jeromemayne.com.

Made in the USA
Columbia, SC
01 July 2019